"If you are looking for practical help in having meaningful family activities that foster togetherness and teach children meaningful lessons, this is your book."

Gary D. Chapman, PhD
Author of *The Five Love Languages*

"Tim Smith can help build a legacy of faith for your family. The most effective Christian education takes place in the home, but most families are looking for good material to use at family time. Tim's ideas are practical, experiential, fun, and life transforming. I highly recommend you have a regular family time and start with this book."

Jim Burns, PhD
President, HomeWord

"Tim Smith has done it again! He has delivered to the harried parent a hands-on guide to strengthen the key relationship between moms and dads and their children. Every parent, or grandparent as in my case, holding this book has the opportunity to intentionally speak a blessing into our kids by giving them our greatest asset: our time. When we invest time in our kids it will pay great dividends. If you are short on ideas, Tim Smith is the man to give them to you."

Dr. Gary and Barb Rosberg
America's Family Coaches and authors of *The 5 Love Needs of Men and Women*

"Here's a chance to turn off the TV and do something fun and fruitful together as a family! Fifty-two great ideas that help bring Christ back into the center of your home as a family."

Mark A. Holmen
Sr. Pastor, Ventura Missionary Church and author of *Faith Begins at Home*

Other Resources by Timothy Smith

Books

*Connecting With Your Kids: How Fast Families Can Move From
Chaos to Closeness*
*The Danger of Raising Nice Kids: Preparing Your Children to
Change Their World*
Family Traditions: Strengthening Your Family Identity and Unity

Audio Book

The Relaxed Parent: Helping Your Kids Do More As You Do Less

52 FAMILY TIME IDEAS

*Draw closer to your kids
as you draw your kids
closer to God*

Timothy Smith

BETHANYHOUSE

MINNEAPOLIS, MINNESOTA

Published by Bethany House Publishers
11400 Hampshire Avenue South
Bloomington, Minnesota 55438

Bethany House Publishers is a division of
Baker Publishing Group, Grand Rapids, Michigan.

Printed in the United States of America

ISBN-13:   978-0-7642-0240-7
ISBN-10:   0-7642-0240-5

Library of Congress Cataloging-in-Publication Data

Smith, Tim, 1954-
    52 family time ideas : draw close to your kids as you draw your kids closer to God / Timothy Smith.
        p.   cm.
    Summary: "Presents fifty-two activity plans for parents who desire weekly family time. Most lessons are intended to last twenty minutes and include a suggested Bible reading, activity, discussion, and prayer. Written for families with children from ages four to fourteen"—Provided by publisher.
    ISBN-13: 987-0-7642-0240-7 (pbk).
    ISBN-10: 0-7642-0240-5 (pbk.)
    1. Family—Religious life.   I. Title.   II. Title: Fifty-two family time ideas.
    BV4526.3.S64   2006
    249—dc22   2006019412

To Nicole and Brooke

TIMOTHY SMITH is a family coach, speaker, president of Life Skills for American Families, and the author of several books. He is a research fellow with the George H. Gallup International Institute and a radio commentator. Tim and his wife have two young-adult daughters and live in Southern California.

Timothy Smith does keynote speaking and presents at family conferences and parenting seminars throughout North America. He also makes presentations in the workplace on work/home balance and wellness issues related to family life. You can reach Tim by calling toll free at 877-376-3500 or by writing Life Skills for American Families at P.O. Box 7736, Thousand Oaks, CA 91360.

contents

PART TWO: Special Occasions and Holidays

Start Here

Ever promise your children you'd take them to an amusement park? They may be excited for days—until you get there! Then as they gaze up at the roller coaster, or the spinning gizmo, or the animal-shaped car that disappears into a dark tunnel—they become afraid.

I want you to experience the same thing!

Not because I'm mean, but because it will be fun.

Really!

Taking the step to have a weekly family time might be a little scary at first—most adventures are—but don't worry. You won't be alone. I will be your guide. You won't get lost, and I'll make sure you don't eat too much cotton candy before going on the whirling teacups. In other words, you'll be okay.

52 Family Time Ideas is a journey of discovery, together. That means it will be fun. But like a thrilling amusement ride, it will require a little risk. It will be a journey—going to a place you have never been before. The good news is you won't even have to take the minivan! And you get to do it together.

Today's families don't seem to have much time for each other, and if we finally carve out time, we twiddle our thumbs, look at each other, and ask, "So waddya wanna do?"

52 Family Time Ideas provides the structure and ideas for the meaningful and fun family time you want, helping you to discover and experience God's timeless principles for strong families.

In just twenty minutes each week you will discover treasures right in your own family. You will also be building lasting memories for you and your children.

I pray that these sessions will launch a tradition of love, laughter, and learning together for your family, because *families really matter.*

A Few Tips to Get You Started

1. Set aside time each week. If you can, make it the same time from week to week. Children benefit from routine and will anticipate the time. If you choose a weekend Family Time, you may need to be flexible with other activities.

2. Read the weekly session ahead of time and obtain the materials you will need. (A **Master Materials List** that summarizes what's needed for all the sessions is also in the back of the book.) You might even practice reading the Scripture text for maximum expression and impact.

3. Protect your Family Time by eliminating any distractions like the phone, TV, radio, video games, or the computer. You will need about twenty minutes for the regular sessions and one and a half to two hours for Movie Nights.

4. To customize each session for younger children or teenagers, read and think through the sections that start with **Adapting for . . .**

5. Show honor to each other by having every family member present (if possible).

6. Be flexible, and make it fun. Don't worry if your Family Time turns into a laugh-fest; it doesn't have to be a serious "Bible Study." Remember, it's not church—it's family!

Here's to family closeness,

Tim Smith
Thousand Oaks, California

Each session offers the following elements, sometimes in a different order:

Materials Needed—To help the parent prepare.

Main Point—For focus.

Warm-up—To engage the children with a soft start.

Bible Readings—To be read aloud from *New Living Translation* or *The Message*. Even better, use your own Bible. (Can also be used as a Memory Verse.)

Today's Slogan—To be repeated aloud as a fun, simple way to reinforce the aim.

Activity—A fun, active experience using things you have around the house; typically takes ten minutes. Occasional Movie Nights will take longer.

Family Discussion—A few questions to go deeper on the topic and to encourage transfer of learning and accountability. You'll also see subsections that ask, "What Does the Bible Say?" and "What Should We Do?"

Adapting for . . .—Suggestions for younger children (preschool and primary age) and teens.

Prayer—Family Time ends with a prayer that can be read aloud.

Journal—As space permits, a place to record prayers or memories.

Option Plays

There are five ways to use *52 Family Time Ideas*. You don't have to stick with one way—you can mix it up if you like. Just as a skilled quarterback in football might call an option play—pass, hand off, or run it himself—busy parents need options.

1. **Weekly**—Pick a time that works best for your family. It doesn't have to be at night. It could be after pancakes on Saturday. You will need extra time for the Movie Nights. One family did the Movie Nights on Friday night and their other Family Time on Sunday afternoons, right after lunch.

2. **Family Weekend**—Get away for the weekend or go camping in the back yard! Design your own family retreat by choosing three or four Family Times and adding in some fun like swimming, biking, hiking, or late-night bowling.

3. **Vacation**—Dozens of our field-testing families reported that *52 Family Time Ideas* worked great when they were on their summer vacation. Since they were traveling and away from their church, they were able to have spiritual times every day—in just twenty minutes a day. Try to adapt the family time to fit the unique setting of the place you are visiting.

4. **Daily**—Hundreds of our field-testing families participated every day as part of a community or church campaign for thirty to forty days. This takes extra planning because the days come around so quickly, so try to prepare your materials in advance. Try gathering one week's worth of materials at a time.

5. **Holidays Only**—You may be too busy or have other activities or customs with your family, but you are looking for something new to do as a family for holidays and special occasions. Add some substance to Back to School, the New Year, and Independence Day by integrating the holiday sessions from *52 Family Time Ideas*.

If you have some ideas or stories you'd like to share about your Family Time, e-mail me at *tdwrdsmith@aol.com*.

PART ONE

WEEKLY SESSIONS

WHY FAMiLiES?

Main Point: God placed us in families to learn about Him, life, and love.

Materials Needed: Socks, bowls, and string

Warm-up

Ask: "Do parents ever get the day off? What would happen if parents took off for one day and did just what we wanted to—sleep in, don't go to work, play video games, or watch sports all day?"

Bible Reading: Read aloud Deuteronomy 5:7–10. It's good for children to see you read your own Bible—or they can read from theirs—but if this is not possible, read from here:

No other gods, only me. No carved gods of any size, shape, or form of anything whatever, whether of things that fly or walk or swim. Don't bow down to them and don't serve them because I am God, your God, and I'm a most jealous God. I hold parents responsible for any sins they pass on to their children to the third, and yes, even to the fourth generation. But I'm lovingly loyal to the thousands who love me and keep my commandments. (THE MESSAGE)

Family Discussion

God placed us in families to learn about Him, life, and love.
1. **Ask:** "Why does God warn, 'No other gods, only me'?"
(God deserves first place in our lives.)
2. **Ask:** "God expects parents to tell their kids about the true
God. How do parents do that?" (By *telling* their kids about the
real God in contrast to the fake gods that humans create. Parents also *show* what God is like by being kind and cooperative,
obedient to God, and setting an example themselves of what
they are trying to teach their kids.)

Today's Slogan: "God comes first in my life." (Repeat several
times, together.)

Activity: Bowls of Mercy Sock Toss

Get ten clean pairs of socks and roll each up in a ball. Get ten
bowls of various sizes. Tape a number (1 to 10) on each bowl.
Make a line with string at least three feet away from the bowls.
One at a time, each family member stands behind the line and
tosses ten sock balls, one at a time, trying to land one in each
bowl. Keep score.

Adapting for . . .

Younger Children
For the Family Discussion, **Ask:** "We learn about love and
God in our family. When do you feel loved?" After the Activity, skip the Wrap-up but **Say:** "Families that love each other
try to help each other be good by putting God first."

Teens
Move the line of string back to six feet away from the bowls.

During the Wrap-up time, **Ask:** "What would happen in a family that didn't have any rules? What would it be like if lying, stealing, and being mean was okay?"

Wrap-up

1. **Ask:** "What was it like trying to land a sock in each bowl?"

What Does the Bible Say?
2. **Say:** "The ten bowls represent God's Ten Commandments, and today's Scripture is one of those commandments. The first few verses talk about putting God first in our lives. This isn't easy because we'd rather put ourselves first. Trying to land a sock in each bowl is hard to do too. But there is a reward . . ."
3. **Ask:** "What promise does God make to those who love Him and keep His commandments?" (That He will be lovingly loyal to them.)

What Should We Do?
4. **Ask:** "What are some ways we put God first in our lives?" (By thinking of Him first; by knowing what He says and obeying Him; and by wanting to know Him more than wanting to get something.)

Prayer: *Dear heavenly Father, you are awesome and powerful, and you alone deserve first place in our lives. Help us to remember today that you come first. In Jesus' name, Amen.*

WE NEED REMiNDERS

Main Point: Families remind each other of the good things about each other and about God.

Materials Needed: A ball of yarn

Warm-up

Have everyone describe a time when they forgot something. (Hear two or three examples.) **Say:** "It is easy to forget. As a family, we can help each other remember important things."

Bible Reading: Read aloud Deuteronomy 6:6–9:

Write these commandments that I've given you today on your hearts. Get them inside of you and then get them inside your children. Talk about them wherever you are, sitting at home or walking in the street; talk about them from the time you get up in the morning to when you fall into bed at night. Tie them on your hands and foreheads as a reminder; inscribe them on the doorposts of your homes and on your city gates. (THE MESSAGE)

Family Discussion

What Does the Bible Say?

1. **Ask:** "Why does God want us to remember His command-ments?" (So we will obey them.)

What Should We Do?

2. **Ask:** "What are the different ways parents help their kids learn and remember God's commandments?" (Memorize; talk about them as you sit or walk—in the morning and at bed-time; attach them to your head and hands and around the house.)

Today's Slogan: "Good things are worth remembering." (Repeat several times.)

Activity: Spider Web

Holding a ball of yarn, have everyone stand in a circle, spaced about four feet from each other. (This works best with four or more people.) Hold the end of the yarn and **Say:** "Whoever catches the ball has to say two things—something good that he likes about the person who threw the ball and something good about God."

Everyone hangs on to the yarn with one hand and tosses the ball of yarn with the other. Soon you will have a spider web of affirmation and gratefulness.

After several tosses, **Say:** "You can also say what you are thankful for." Continue until you have a beautiful spider web pattern. **Ask**, "What does this web do to us?" (Holds us together; makes us a team.)

Adapting for . . .

Younger Children
Simplify the activity with the instruction: **Say:** "Whoever catches the ball has to say one nice thing about the person they are throwing it to."

Teens
Extend the Discussion and **Ask:** "Which of these faith-building exercises works best with you? Memorizing, sitting and talking about them, thinking about them on walks in the morning; at meals, or at bedtime?" Extend the Activity and **Ask:** "What happens if somebody drops his yarn?" (It ruins the web and makes us weak.)

    Note: After a few sessions, ask your teen to handle leading part or all of a session. We have found that if teens are involved in this way, they tend to get more out of Family Times because they aren't "treated like a kid."

Prayer: *Dear heavenly Father, help us to remember the important things you have done, and who you are. Help us also to remember each other and be thankful for one another; knowing that together we are strong. In Christ's name, Amen.*

FAMiLY TRADiTiONS

Main Point: Our family strength and unity comes from God.

Materials Needed: Broomstick, twine, tape, and paper

Warm-up

Ask: "What are some different kinds of tests?" (Tests at school; skills tests; tryouts to make an athletic team; driver's test; tests to get into some schools, etc.) "What do tests and tryouts show?" (What we know and what we can do.)

Bible Reading: Read aloud Deuteronomy 8:2, 11–14:

Remember every road that God led you on for those forty years in the wilderness, pushing you to your limits, testing you so that he would know what you were made of, whether you would keep his commandments or not. . . . Make sure you don't forget God, your God, by not keeping his commandments, his rules and regulations that I command you today. Make sure that when you eat and are satisfied, build pleasant houses and settle in, see your herds and flocks flourish and more and more money come in, watch your standard of living going up and up—make sure you don't become so full of yourself and your things that you forget God, your God. (THE MESSAGE)

Family Discussion

What Does the Bible Say?
1. **Ask:** "Why does God test us?" (To help us get stronger; to learn to depend on Him.)

What Should We Do?
2. **Ask:** "Why would it be easy to forget God if life was going really well?" (We feel we don't need Him and look to our stuff and money for security.)

Today's Slogan: "We are strong when we pull together."

Activity: Let's Pull Together

(This works best on carpet.) Gather a 3– to 4–foot piece of dowel, broomstick, yardstick, or mop handle; twine; a piece of paper; marker; and tape. On the paper, write the slogan in big letters and tape it to the side of the stick, about two inches from one end. Cut the twine into six-foot pieces—one for each family member. **Say:** "The stick, twine, and slogan represent our family unity. We need to pull together if we are going to stand together in difficult times (as the Hebrews did in the wilderness)." Have each person tie her string a little above the halfway point of the stick. Lay the stick down on the floor and gather the family in a circle around it. Each person holds the end of his or her string. **Ask** one child, "Try to raise the stick and stand it up on end by pulling on your string." (It won't work.) Ask two children to try to raise the stick by pulling. (It might work.) Then **Say:** "Let's all pull together." The object of the activity is to stand the stick up straight with each person maintaining tension on the stick with their string. The stick should stand up. **Say:** "With everyone doing his or her part, we are able to stand tall against the challenges." **Ask:** "What happens if one person isn't connected?" (Let go of your string. The stick will drop or fall.) **Say:** "Everybody is needed in this family. We are strong when we pull together."

Adapting for . . .

Younger Children

Skip Warm-up question 2. For the Activity, sit on the floor in a circle with your feet surrounding the stick. Make the stick shorter, two to three feet in length. If they can't pull the stick up, try standing it up with your hand and holding it up with the strings. Preschool children often don't have the coordination for precise pulling and balance, so help them succeed at making the stick stand up straight.

Teens

After the Activity, have your teen describe a time when you need to pull together as a family. (Example: "When I'm learning to drive, you shouldn't make fun of me.")

Prayer: *Dear heavenly Father, thank you that we have each other. Help us to learn all that we can from the tests of life. Help us to support each other so that we can be strong and stand straight in the middle of life's tests. In Jesus' name, Amen.*

SAND CASTLES OR MONUMENTS?

Main Point: A child's curiosity provides opportunities to teach spiritual truths.

Materials Needed: Twelve smooth river stones (3 to 4 inches each) and permanent (or washable) markers

Warm-up

Ask: "Remember when we visited [the lake] and the water washed over our sand castle? What happens if we build a sand castle too close to the water?" (The water comes up and knocks it down.) "How long would it last if we built it far away from the waves?" (A few days.) "What's a better building material than sand?" (Rocks, bricks, wood, etc., because they last.)

Bible Reading: Read aloud Joshua 4:4–7:

So Joshua called together the twelve men and told them, "Go into the middle of the Jordan, in front of the Ark of the Lord your God. Each of you must pick up one stone and carry it out on your shoul- der—twelve stones in all, one for each of the twelve tribes. We will use these stones to build a memorial. In the future, your children will ask, 'What do these stones mean to you?' Then you can tell them, 'They remind us that the Jordan River stopped flowing when the Ark of the Lord's covenant went across.' These stones will stand as a permanent memorial among the people of Israel."

Family Discussion

What Does the Bible Say?

1. **Ask:** "Why do you think God told them to use stones?" (Because they last longer than sand, and they were readily available.)

2. **Ask:** "What were the stones for?" (To remind us that the Jordan River stopped flowing and the Ark of the Lord's covenant went across the dry riverbed.)

What Should We Do?

3. **Ask:** "What are some ways we can use stones or rocks to help us remember the miracles God did for His people?" (Write on rocks and leave them around the house or garden.)

Today's Slogan: "A faith that rocks is one that remembers."

Activity: The Rocks Cry Out

Purchase twelve smooth river stones (about 3 to 4 inches each) from your home improvement center or garden supply store. Divide the rocks evenly among the family members. **Ask:** "What are some ways God has been faithful to us?" One at a time, have each person explain how he or she has seen God at work. Then, using permanent markers, write on the stones how God has been faithful to your family. After you are finished, display your rocks inside or in the garden as a memorial and tribute to God's work in your family.

Adapting for . . .

Younger Children
Instead of describing in words, younger kids can draw pictures of what they are thankful for on the rocks. Don't use permanent markers. Use washable markers.

Teens
Ask: "How will you explain the rock garden to your friends when they come over?" and "What should we name our rock garden?" Ask them if they would like to make a sign with the name.

Prayer: *Thank you, God, that you remember us. You never forget about us. We are precious in your sight. Help us to remember all that you have done for us. In the name of your Son, Jesus, Amen.*

LOVE DOESN'T QUiT
(MOViE NiGHT)

Main Point: Love never gives up.

Materials Needed: Rent or buy the movie *Finding Nemo*.

Warm-up

Pop some popcorn and get cozy around the TV. **Say:** "Can you think of three stories that show that love never gives up?" (Any story will do, but you could also mention that God's story is a love story too!)

Bible Reading: Read aloud 1 Corinthians 13:4–7:

Love is patient and kind. Love is not jealous or boastful or proud or rude. Love does not demand its own way. Love is not irritable, and it keeps no record of when it has been wronged. It is never glad about injustice but rejoices whenever the truth wins out. Love never gives up, never loses faith, is always hopeful, and endures through every circumstance. (EMPHASIS ADDED)

Activity: *Finding Nemo*

Introduce the movie and **Say:** "Tonight we are going to watch a movie about the love between a father and a son; the kind of love that withstands all kinds of problems."

Time-saver: If you don't have time to see the entire movie, watch as much as you can and then skip to the "Reunion" scene near the end (scene 29 on DVD). Adjust the Family Discussion accordingly.

Family Discussion

1. **Ask:** "What part of the movie did you like?"
2. **Ask:** "What do you think Nemo learned about his father's love for him?"
3. **Ask:** "What did Nemo's dad do to show his love for his son?" (Crossed the ocean to search for his son.)
4. **Ask:** "Nemo's dad (Marlin) was really protective of his son. What are some ways human parents protect their children?"

Today's Slogan: "Love never gives up."

Adapting for . . .

Younger Children

Skip the Warm-up question and begin with the Scripture, followed by your introduction of the movie. You may choose to show only part of the movie to accommodate the attention span of preschool-age children. Or you may prefer to show the movie in multiple sittings. After the movie, skip Discussion questions 2 and 4.

Teens
After the movie, have your teen describe a time when parents AND teens need to hang in there and not give up.

Prayer: *Dear heavenly Father, thank you for your love that never gives up on us. Even with problems and bad things, your love never gives up. You sent Jesus to this planet so we could be with you. Thank you that you go great distances to show your love for us. In Jesus' name, Amen.*

J O U R N A L
RECORD YOUR FAMiLY TiME MEMORiES
& EXPERiENCES HERE

FAMiLY IS STiLL A GOOD IDEA

Main Point: The family is God's idea.

Materials Needed: Park with playground equipment or indoor mall if the weather is too severe; toy blocks or dominoes

Warm-up

Ask: "How would life be different if there were no families?" (Entertain a few responses, even some wild ones.)

Bible Reading: Read aloud Deuteronomy 7:9:

Understand, therefore, that the Lord your God is indeed God. He is the faithful God who keeps his covenant for a thousand generations and constantly loves those who love him and obey his commands.

Family Discussion

What Does the Bible Say?

Say: "God designed the family so that parents can help their children know the truth about Him and His world. It's the parents' job to help their children know and love God." (Line up several blocks in a row.)

Ask: "Do you know what a generation is?" (Parents are one generation, their kids are the next generation, and when they become parents their kids will be the third generation.) Indicate three generations with three blocks. You can set them up like dominoes, so they will knock each other over as you touch the one on the end.

What Should We Do?

Ask: "How can God pass on His love to a thousand generations?" (One parent and one child at a time.) **Say:** "Today we will see how parents can pass on something good to their children and they can pass it on to their kids. It's a chain of good things."

Today's Slogan: "Family is a good idea because it's God's idea."

Activity: Playground Parable

Go to a neighborhood park or playground that has swings or climbing apparatus. Spend fifteen minutes climbing, hanging, swinging, and sliding. Try playing Follow the Leader and have a child be the leader—everyone has to copy what he does—including the parents! Try to emphasize that in families we follow the leader and we pass on good things to the younger ones.

Adapting for . . .

Younger Children

Choose a park with equipment designed for preschoolers. If weather doesn't permit outdoor activity, go to a mall that has indoor playground equipment.

Teens

Go to the park at night so there's less of a chance that your teen's friends will see him or her! Afterward, reward them with an ice-cream cone. If weather doesn't permit, then consider doing another indoor activity where you can "follow" each other, like ice-skating, roller-skating, bowling, or scaling an indoor climbing wall.

Prayer: *Dear Father God, we praise you for making our family. We praise you for including us in your family. Thank you for making us part of the chain of blessing for a thousand generations. We will be careful to pass on your love. In Jesus' name, Amen.*

THE WORRY-HURRY CONNECTiON

Main Point: We need to stop ourselves from always being in a hurry.

Materials Needed: Red construction paper, scissors, markers, and tape. Some kids are very slow paper cutters, up to second or third grade, so it might be good to plan on cutting out the octagons beforehand, providing stencils, or tracing them on paper.

Warm-up

Say: "Today we are going to slow down, sit in one place, and have time for one another, but it's going to be kind of weird. We are going to have a staring contest!" Sit in a circle on the floor. Look each person in the eye and stare. Try not to blink. "If you blink, you are eliminated from the circle."

Bible Reading: Read aloud Philippians 4:6–7:

Don't worry about anything; instead, pray about everything. Tell God what you need, and thank Him for all He has done. If you do this, you will experience God's peace, which is far more wonderful than the human mind can understand. His peace will guard your hearts and minds as you live in Christ Jesus.

Family Discussion

Say: "In this Family Time we start looking at reasons why we are in such a hurry. Today's reason is that *our culture likes a fast pace*. Nobody likes to go slow. It seems like we are becoming more and more hurried."

What Does the Bible Say?
Ask: "Instead of worrying, what are we supposed to do?" (Pray)

What Should We Do?
Ask: "Do you think our family is in a hurry very often? When does that happen?"
Ask: "How does our modern world make it possible for us to do things fast? "What are some of the things we do that are fast?" (Fast food, drive-thru's, microwave dinners, computers, overnight deliveries, downloading music, e-mail, etc.)
Ask: "Is it always good to be in a hurry? When is it better to slow down?"

Today's Slogan: "God's peace helps us not to need to hurry."

Activity: Stop Signs

Using construction paper, scissors, and markers, make an octagon to be used for a stop sign. Discuss phrases from Scripture that might help us stop the hurry, and write them on your signs (for example, under "STOP," write "Don't Worry!" or "Pray!" etc.) Post these around the house as reminders to focus on God's peace and not always be rushing.

Adapting for . . .

Younger Children

Early writers might enjoy having their signs pre-made with the words very lightly written or done in dots for them to trace. Shorten the discussion and **Ask:** "When do you like to go fast?" and "When do you like to go slow or stop?" For the Activity, pre-cut the stop signs.

Teens

Ask: "Why is it important for you to obey traffic signs as you learn to drive?" and "What might happen if all teen drivers ignored traffic signs and signals?" Ask them to post the stop sign in their room as a reminder to ask God for peace when they feel stressed or rushed.

Prayer: *Help us, God, not to be in such a hurry that we don't take time for one another. Help us to take time to talk with you about everything, so we can have your peace in our hearts and minds. In Jesus' name, Amen.*

ESCAPE FROM HURRY AT WORK AND SCHOOL

Main Point: Speed doesn't always work as well at home.

Materials Needed: Baby food, spoon, juice, sipper cup, and bib

---

Warm-up

Ask: "What was your least favorite baby food? What was your favorite?" (If the child doesn't remember, Mom could probably recall.)

Bible Reading: Read aloud 1 Thessalonians 2:7–8:

We were as gentle among you as a mother feeding and caring for her own children. We loved you so much that we gave you not only God's Good News but our own lives, too.

Family Discussion

1. **Ask:** "Have you noticed that you can't hurry babies when they are eating?" (Some kids may not have noticed this.) **Say:** "One thing I learned when you were babies is that you can't be hurried. You liked to take your time with the bottle and enjoy each swallow. As you got older, you liked to *experience* your food; not necessarily eat it! Sometimes it got in your hair, on the walls, on the floor, and a little bit actually got in your mouth!" **Ask:** "Why do you think you can't rush babies?"
2. **Ask:** "Do you ever feel rushed to finish your work at school?"

What Does the Bible Say?
3. **Ask:** "Why is it important to be gentle when feeding and caring for babies?" (We shouldn't always rush; instead, we should take time to care for one another and give one another what we need.)

What Should We Do?
4. **Ask:** "Are there some things that we do that are hurried or rushed? What are some things that we might do better or enjoy more if we slowed down?" (Example: family meals)

Today's Slogan: "Doing things faster isn't always better."

Activity: Big Baby

Do a role reversal and have your kids feed *you* baby food and juice from a sipper cup. Make sure you wear a bib. Have them feed you as fast as they can spoon it up. After a jar of baby food, debrief with them about the experience. **Ask:** "Was it fun? Weird? Aren't you glad we don't do that every day?" etc.

Adapting for . . .

Younger Children
Skip questions 3 and 4 in the Discussion. If your child is at least four years old, she should be able to do this Activity. If she is younger, have one parent feed the other. If there is only one parent, feed yourself! Then discuss what she thought about watching you.

Teens
They are going to love this activity as is! Wear old clothes.

Prayer: *Dear Father God, help us not to always be in a hurry. Give us patience and understanding at home, school, and work. Help us to make time for one another because we love each other. In Jesus' name, Amen.*

J O U R N A L
RECORD YOUR FAMiLY TiME MEMORiES
& EXPERiENCES HERE

IT TAKES TiME TO GROW UP

Main Point: There is nothing *instant* about maturity.

Materials Needed: Pencil, butcher paper (or heavy-duty plain wrapping paper), scissors, and markers

Warm-up

With a pencil, mark everyone's height on a doorjamb. **Ask:** "Can you get taller by wishing you were taller?" (No) **Say:** "Growth takes time. When we get older, it's called becoming 'mature.' We grow physically—get taller and bigger—but what are some other ways we grow?" (Emotionally, mentally, etc.)

Bible Reading: Read aloud Ephesians 4:10–15:

[God] handed out gifts above and below, filled heaven with his gifts, filled earth with his gifts. He handed out gifts of apostle, prophet, evangelist, and pastor-teacher to train Christians in skilled servant work, working within Christ's body, the church, until we're all moving rhythmically and easily with each other, efficient and graceful in response to God's Son, fully mature adults, fully developed within and without, fully alive like Christ. No prolonged infancies among us, please. We'll not tolerate babes in the woods, small children who are an easy mark for impostors. God wants us to grow up, to know the whole truth and tell it in love—like Christ in everything. (THE MESSAGE, EMPHASIS ADDED)

Check to make sure your child understands the more difficult words in the Bible Reading, such as *rhythmically, prolonged,* and *tolerate.*

Family Discussion

What Does the Bible Say?

1. **Ask:** "What does God give us to help us grow up?" (Each other, to help each other; everyone has a position to play on God's team.)

2. **Ask:** "What are some things that help us grow physically?" (Good food, plenty of sleep, exercise, clean water.) "Can we see the growth right away? If I eat my vegetables tonight, will I be bigger and stronger in the morning?" (No)

What Should We Do?

3. **Ask:** "What do we need to grow with each other as a family?" (Time together, to be kind to one another, a safe home, to protect one another. These take time, and added together over the years make a healthy home. It takes time to grow a family.)

Today's Slogan: "Growing up isn't baby stuff."

Activity: Good Giant

Using a pencil and butcher or wrapping paper, trace the tallest person in your family by having them lie on the paper. Then make him or her taller by adding a few inches to the neck and legs. Have each family member think of one thing that will help the giant grow physically and draw that on or near him (vegetables, milk, etc.). Also have each family member think of one thing that will help the giant grow in maturity and character (by getting along with others, being kind, protecting others from harm, saying nice things, not running in the house or yelling inside, etc.).

Display the giant where you will see him as a reminder that it's important to grow up.

Adapting for . . .

Younger Children

During the Discussion, skip question 3. For the Activity, simplify the Discussion and **Ask:** "What do kids need to grow big?" (Milk, vegetables, fruit, meat, sleep, exercise, etc.)

Teens

For older teens, you may want to skip the Activity and extend the Discussion and **Ask:** "The Bible talks about growing up with truth and love. Why is truth and love essential for growing up?" As an alternative activity, you could make a poster of the things we need to grow up. Draw a stick figure with dialogue bubbles (like comics use) of several essentials for growing up.

Prayer: *God, help us to grow up and not be babies. Help us to be mature and know the truth and tell it in love. In Jesus' name, Amen.*

LEARNiNG CONTENTMENT

Main Point: Contentment makes me flexible.

Materials Needed: Dictionary, a can of peaches, spoons, bowls, and can opener

Warm-up

Ask: "What is something that you would like right now as a gift?" (A toy, doll, motorcycle, clothes, etc.) "Where did you learn about this cool thing?" (Probably on TV or from friends.)

Bible Reading: Read aloud Philippians 4:11–12:

Not that I was ever in need, for I have learned how to get along happily whether I have much or little. I know how to live on almost nothing or with everything. I have learned the secret of living in every situation, whether it is with a full stomach or empty, with plenty or little.

Family Discussion

Say: "There's nothing wrong with wanting cool things like toys, bikes, and clothes, but when we want things too much, it can lead to problems."

What Does the Bible Say?
1. **Ask:** "Contentment means to learn how to get along happily with little or much. It's the 'being full' feeling instead of feeling empty. Can you think of a time when you felt this way?"

What Should We Do?
2. Look up *contentment* in the dictionary and discuss it. **Ask:** "How does contentment help us at home?" (We learn to be happy with what we have and to be thankful for it.)

Today's Slogan: "Happy with little or happy with much, makes me happy."

Activity: Contented Peaches

Get a can of peaches, can opener, bowls, and spoons. Pass around the can and call attention to the "contents" on the label. For example, it might say, "24 ounces of peaches in their own juice." Food products are required to have the content description on the label. **Ask:** "What would you think if we opened this can of peaches and there were snails inside?" Open the can. **Ask:** "How would you feel if the can was half empty? This can is full." Show that it is full. "We are content when we are full. When we focus on what we don't have, we are not content, but whiny and wanting." Spoon up the peaches into bowls and enjoy!

Adapting for . . .

Younger Children
Skip the Discussion and **Ask:** "Sometimes we have to stop wanting and just be happy with what we have. What do you have that makes you happy?"

Teens
After the Activity, **Ask:** "What can we do to remind ourselves to be content and not whine about what we don't have?" (Examples: demonstrate with a glass of milk half full, etc.)

Prayer: *Dear heavenly Father, help us to be satisfied with what we have and not be running after the latest thing we think we must have. In Jesus' name, Amen.*

J O U R N A L
RECORD YOUR FAMiLY TiME MEMORiES & EXPERiENCES HERE

THE POWER OF NOT GiViNG UP (MOViE NiGHT)

Main Point: God gives us strength not to give up.

Materials Needed: *Father of the Bride* movie, or as an alternative for younger children, try *Eight Below*.

Warm-up

Pop some popcorn and gather around the TV. **Ask:** "What are some things that we get better at if we keep trying?" (Building blocks, learning to ride a bike, coloring, toilet training, sports, etc.) **Ask:** "What does it take to get better at something?" (Practice, doing it over and over, and a willingness to learn.)

Bible Reading: Read aloud Philippians 4:13:

For I can do everything with the help of Christ who gives me the strength I need.

What Does the Bible Say?
Ask: "What can we do with Christ's help?" (Everything!)

Activity: *Father of the Bride*

Enjoy the movie together. Take a few minutes at the end to discuss the film. If you watch *Eight Below* or another movie, adjust the Family Discussion accordingly.

Family Discussion

What Should We Do?
1. **Ask:** "Today's session is about not giving up. In the movie we saw several scenes of a person not giving up, like the scene at the pool when the father of the bride was trying to get the man's wallet and the dogs were after him. What were some other scenes that showed someone not giving up?" (Planning the wedding, trying to see his daughter during the wedding, etc.)
2. **Ask:** "What are some things that you have to do that are difficult and make you feel like giving up?" (Homework, cleaning my room, yard work)

Today's Slogan: "God's strength helps me not to give up."

Adapting for . . .

Younger Children
Eight Below may be too long for some, so substitute a shorter video designed for preschoolers that deals with the theme of working hard, finishing a task, or not giving up (for example, *Bob the Builder: Getting the Job Done*). Talk about the movie,

then **Ask:** "What are some things that are hard to do, but you can do them now because you kept trying?" (Learned to tie my shoes, dress myself, stack blocks, pick up my toys, etc.)

Teens
This time, the teens get to ask the questions. **Ask** Mom or Dad to "describe a time when you were persistent and hung in there, against the odds." **Ask:** "What made the difference? Why didn't you give up?"

Prayer: (If you want to, mention some of the needs that were discussed from Discussion question 2.) *Dear heavenly Father, sometimes we feel like giving up. We feel like quitting. Give us your strength to hang in there.* (Example: Give Jennifer the strength to study for her test. . . .)

WWF—WORLD WRESTLiNG FAMiLiES

Main Point: Sometimes our selfishness causes fights.

Materials Needed: Paper and pen

Warm-up

For the parent(s) to answer: "What did you do as a child to scheme to get your way?" (If you cannot recall anything, or if your example is not appropriate, create or find such a story.)

Bible Reading: Read aloud James 4:1–3:

What is causing the quarrels and fights among you? Isn't it the whole army of evil desires at war within you? You want what you don't have, so you scheme and kill to get it. You are jealous for what others have, and you can't possess it, so you fight and quarrel to take it away from them. And yet the reason you don't have what you want is that you don't ask God for it. And even when you do ask, you don't get it because your whole motive is wrong—you want only what will give you pleasure.

Family Discussion

1. **Ask:** "Besides air, water, and sun, what would be hard to live without?" (List the items on a large sheet of paper) **Ask:** "What do you need to get through the day?"

What Does the Bible Say?
2. Reread today's verses and **Ask:** "Sometimes what we want gets in the way of getting along with others. What are some of the problems listed in the Scripture?" (Fighting, evil desires, scheming, killing, jealousy)

What Should We Do?
3. **Ask:** "What makes life comfortable for you?" (Write down the answers and expand the list until you have at least a dozen comfort-producing things: blow-dryer, bed, MP3 player, etc.)

Today's Slogan: "The most important things in life aren't things."

Activity: Family Survivor

Say: "Imagine that our plane crashed in the warm waters of the South Pacific. Our family alone survived. We are in a life raft with all of this stuff (point to the list just written) and it's too heavy. If we are going to make it to the island a mile away, we have to get rid of the extra baggage. What would you get rid of first? And you can't say, 'My little brother.'"

Each person takes turns crossing off one item and explains why they chose that one. Accept their decision. Explain that there shouldn't be arguing. Keep taking turns until there is only one item left. Discuss why the final item is important to the family.

Adapting for . . .

Younger Children

Instead of the Survivor story (too scary for little ones), **Ask:** "Let's say you are going to visit Grandma or a friend for the night. What would you want to put in your backpack (or overnight bag)? What would you *need* to take?"

Teens

Extend the Discussion and **Ask:** "What are some ways life is like a life raft, forcing us to make hard choices?" (We don't have time or money to do all that we want to do. Some choices compete against each other.)

Prayer: *Father God, help us to remember that people are more important than things. Teach us not to be selfish. In Jesus' name, Amen.*

J O U R N A L
RECORD YOUR FAMiLY TiME MEMORiES & EXPERiENCES HERE

WHY WE RUSH

Main Point: We rush for many reasons; most of them are not healthy.

Materials Needed: Car to drive to a health club, sporting goods store, or pet store

Warm-up

Gather the family in one room. Have them wait for you while you go into another room and put on lots of heavy gear (helmet, hiking boots, trench coat, backpack, goggles, etc.). Then come out and **Say:** "I'm ready to run a race! Who wants to race me? Do I look ready to run? Why not?"

Take off each item as you offer a lame reason for wearing it. (For example, "I was going to wear the goggles so bugs wouldn't get into my eyes while I ran.") At the end, **Ask:** "How do you prepare to run?" (By wearing nothing that hinders you or slows you down.)

Bible Reading: Read aloud 1 Corinthians 9:24:

Remember that in a race everyone runs, but only one person gets the prize. You also must run in such a way that you will win.

Family Discussion

What Does the Bible Say?
Ask: "Who runs the race?" (Everyone) "How many win?" (Only one) "What's the trick to winning?" (Be faster than everyone else.)

What Should We Do?
Say: "Here are five *Reasons Why We Rush*: These seem like good ideas, but like the stuff I was wearing for my race, they actually aren't helpful.
1. We like the latest things like toys, music, and fashion.
2. We want to do lots of things in a short amount of time. We hate wasting time.
3. We expect fast service and fast technology (computers, etc.).
4. We, as a family, want to have and do lots of things, but there isn't time to get them all or do them all without hurrying.
5. We are running from something. (We don't want to face the past; we are afraid to slow down and feel; or we are nervous about the future.)"
Ask: "Which of these do you see as a reason/reasons why we (as a family) rush?"

Today's Slogan: "Run to win."

Activity: Tour Treadmills

It's time to get out of the house for a while. Take a quick tour of your health club or request to walk through one in your neighborhood. All you want to look at are the treadmills. Another place you can see them are at sporting goods stores. **Ask** your kids: "Can you get anywhere running on one of these?" Another option is to go to a pet store and watch the hamsters spin around on their wheels. ("You can't run to win if you are running in circles.")

Adapting for . . .

Younger Children

Explain the reasons for rushing in terms they'd understand and provide examples. (Example: "Would you rather be in the front of the line or the back of the line to go down the slide at the park?") Instead of driving somewhere, have your kids run in place and pump their legs faster and faster.

Teens

Extend the Discussion and **Ask:** "Do you think adults are more hurried than teens? Why?" After the Activity, **Ask:** "What are some ways we, as family members, look like hamsters on the wheel or runners on the treadmill, frantically running in place but not getting anywhere? What can we do about it?"

Prayer: *God, help us not to run foolishly just because everyone else is, but to discover the right speed for our family. In Jesus' name, Amen.*

SOLD OUT

Main Point: Our priorities reveal what's in our heart.

Materials Needed: Fake check (you can draw it), butcher paper, pencils, rulers, crayons, and markers

Warm-up

Playact and **Say:** "We just won the magazine sweepstakes! Some guy dropped off a check at our front door for $50,000!" (Show a fake check.) "What should we do with the money?" (Take turns responding. If somebody doesn't suggest it, bring up the idea of fixing up the house.)

Bible Reading: Read aloud Deuteronomy 6:5:

And you must love the Lord your God with all your heart, all your soul, and all your strength.

Family Discussion

1. **Ask:** "If the center of the home is where we hang out the most, what is the center of our home?"
2. **Ask:** "What is your favorite place in your house? Why?"

What Does the Bible Say?
3. **Ask:** "How should we love the Lord?" (With all that we are. All of us.)

What Should We Do?
4. **Ask:** "If we love God completely, it will show in how we act. What can we expect to see in the life of someone who loves God with all that he or she is?" (Likes to sing praises, learn about God, read the Bible, help people in need, etc.)

Today's Slogan: "Loving God demands all of us."

Activity: Home Makeover

Get out butcher paper or white shelf paper, pencils, rulers, and crayons or markers, and cut a two-foot piece of paper for each person. **Say:** "You are going to design your dream house. It can be anything that you want it to be, but you only have four minutes to draw it. Go." When time is up, **Say:** "You now have thirty seconds to describe your dream house." Take turns.

Then **Say:** "Those were great, but they were just *houses*. A cool-looking house is not a home. What makes a home?" (List the ideas on paper, for example: love, patience, kindness, respect, etc.) **Ask:** "How can we illustrate these?" You might want to have these drawn on sticky notes or other small papers to stick or tape onto your house drawing.

Draw a rough blueprint of your present house and take the ideas for illustrating the qualities and place them in various rooms. (Example: Sharing the bathroom requires patience.)

Adapting for . . .

Younger Children

Help them understand the abstract concepts of heart, soul, and strength. For instance, with "heart," we aren't talking about the muscle in our chest that pumps blood. We are thinking of that part of us that wishes and feels. "Soul" is that part of us that loves and worships God, and "strength" is in our bodies and what we can do with them, how we can serve others.

Teens

Deepen the Discussion and **Ask:** "What would a teen look like—behavior-wise and in his choices—who loved God with ALL of his heart, soul, and strength?"

Prayer: *Help us to love you, Lord, with all of our heart, soul, and strength, in every room of our house and in every area of our lives. In Jesus' name, Amen.*

SESSION 15
HEART GUARD

Main Point: We need to protect our heart because it influences our choices.

Materials Needed: Clear glass jar, walnut-sized rocks, marbles, sand, bowls, and masking tape

Warm-up

Ask: "What would you do with an extra three hours each day? Let's say we can magically make each day into a 27-hour day for just our family? What would you do with the extra time?"

Bible Reading: Read aloud Proverbs 4:23:

Keep vigilant watch over your heart; that's where life starts. (THE MESSAGE)

Activity: Time Jar

Gather a clear glass jar (mayonnaise or canning jar), some rocks (about the size of a walnut, or use walnuts), marbles, and sand (or rice). With masking tape or a sticker, label the jar "24 Hours." Before Family Time, fill the jar almost to the top with the rocks; add the marbles; then pour in the sand. Then empty the jar and separate the rocks, marbles, and sand into three bowls.

Gather your children and **Say:** "This is a Time Jar. It represents all of the time we have in one day. The rocks are for the *hard* things we have to do—chores, homework, going to work, practicing the clarinet, etc. The marbles stand for the regular stuff that isn't hard, but we just do in the day—like brush our teeth, eat our vegetables, and get to bed on time. The sand stands for all of the fun stuff we do in a day. The easy things, like playing, watching TV, video games, and eating sweets. Working together we will fill up our Time Jar with what we'd want to do." (Have a few kids take turns filling the jar, describing each activity as you go.)

Then **Say:** "We have to watch what we fill our day with, or we won't fit it all in. If we start by taking care of the harder things (put the rocks in), we will have time for the medium things (put the marbles in) and the fun stuff (put the sand in). But if we start with only the easy and fun stuff, we can't fit it all in."

Family Discussion

1. **Ask:** "What would happen if we filled up our time with nothing but fun stuff?"
2. **Ask:** "Why does it work one way, but not the other? Why can't we do the fun stuff first, and then work in the harder?" (Because it won't fit.)

What Does the Bible Say?

3. **Ask:** "*Vigilant* means 'being careful.' How do we have to be careful about the part of us that wishes and feels?"

What Should We Do?

4. **Ask:** "Protecting our heart means being careful with what we see and do. What are some things around us that are not healthy for our hearts?"

Today's Slogan: "Watch your heart and you'll have a good start."

Adapting for . . .

Younger Children

The concept of the "heart" is too abstract for preschool children. Like in the previous session, remind them that here we aren't talking about the organ that pumps blood, but instead the part of them that wishes and dreams. For a preschool child, the heart is the imagination; it is his "wisher."

Teens

Extend the Discussion and **Ask:** "Where do we see an emphasis on the heart?" (Popular music and culture.) **Ask:** "Why are teens so interested in issues of the heart?" (They are hoping for romance and are dreaming of the future.)

Prayer: *Dear heavenly Father, help us to guard our hearts and have them focused on the right things—those things that are important to you. In Jesus' name, Amen.*

DON'T BREAK MY HEART

Main Point: Healthy families don't crush each other by expecting perfection.

Materials Needed: Tape measure, painter's tape or sticky notes, chalk, candy bar, broomstick, recorded music, and CD player

Warm-up

Get a tape measure and **Ask**, "How high do you think you can jump?" Have your child stand flat-footed next to the wall and stretch his hand up and touch the wall. Mark the highest point with painter's tape or a sticky note.

Coat chalk on his fingertips and **Say:** "Now jump as high as you can and touch above the tape." Measure the distance for his vertical leap. Have everyone in the family repeat.

Then **Say:** "I want you to jump 48 inches." Offer a candy bar to the first one who can jump 48 inches. Let them try. They will get frustrated. **Ask:** "Am I being too hard?"

Then divide up the candy bar and read the Scripture.

Bible Reading: Read aloud Colossians 3:21:

Parents, don't come down too hard on your children or you'll crush their spirits. (THE MESSAGE)

What Does the Bible Say?

Ask: "What does this Bible verse mean?" (That parents shouldn't burden or be hard on their kids by expecting them to be perfect.) You might have to explain "crush their spirits" as discouragement or making a child feel sad or feel bad about himself/herself.

Activity: Limbo

Say: "How low can you go? With a broomstick, try to limbo (bend your back backward and go underneath the stick without touching it or the floor with your hands). If you are successful, the stick is lowered a notch." This will be frustrating and painful to some parents (who don't bend as well), and fun and entertaining to your kids! Play some Caribbean or Hawaiian music if you have it. Everyone should try the limbo at least once.

Family Discussion

1. **Ask:** "What was fun about limbo? What was not fun?" (Falling, being in pain, losing)
2. **Ask:** "What would happen if we had to be really good at limbo or we wouldn't get dessert?" (That would be unfair and frustrating.)

What Should We Do?

3. **Ask:** "Expecting too much from someone can be frustrating to them. It can crush their spirit and discourage them. What are some ways parents are sometimes too hard on their kids?"
4. **Ask:** "Sometimes kids expect their parents to be perfect. Give me an example."

Adapting for . . .

Younger Children
Shorten the Discussion to two questions. Make sure you explain and illustrate terms that may be too complex for them. For example, in the Bible reading, "don't come down too hard on them" doesn't mean parents physically pressure their kids, but it means they smash their hopes.

Teens
Extend the Discussion and **Ask:** "Can teens be too hard on their parents? How?" (By expecting too much, or being unrealistic.)

Today's Slogan: "Keep it hopeful. Keep it real."

Prayer: *Heavenly Father, help us to be realistic with our expectations of each other rather than frustrating. Help us to encourage and support one another. In Jesus' name, Amen.*

HEART TRAINING

Main Point: Expecting too little from our kids can frustrate them.

Materials Needed: Wooden blocks or books, containers of soap bubbles (with wands), a pie tin, flex ties ("twisties"), and pipe cleaners

---

Warm-up

Holding wooden blocks or books, **Say:** "I bet nobody can stack these blocks to make a one-foot tower." Allow a child or two to demonstrate, and then **Say:** "Oh, I guess I was expecting too little of you. How did that make you feel?" (They might say, "Angry, because it was too easy.") (Adjust the height of the tower to accommodate your child's age. If they are eight to ten years old, have them try a four-foot tower.)

Bible Reading: Read aloud Ephesians 6:4:

And now a word to you fathers. Don't make your children angry by the way you treat them. Rather, bring them up with the discipline and instruction approved by the Lord.

What Does the Bible Say?

Say: "If parents aren't careful, we can make our kids angry and frustrated by how we discipline them. Today's Family Time is about getting the right balance with our training."

Activity: Bubble School

Provide a container of bubble soap with a wand for each family member. Pour some of the soap into a pie tin. Make a tiny wand out of flex ties (about 1/2-inch in diameter) and another one out of pipe cleaners (about six inches in diameter). **Say:** "Welcome to Bubble School. Before you open your bubbles, let's do a little research." Ask for volunteers to try to blow bubbles using the tiny wand (it won't work too well, if at all). **Say:** "Perhaps the wand is too small. Let's try the big wand." (Have a few try using the big wand. Unless they are really skilled, this won't work either.) **Say:** "The Bubble Maker knew that most of the time this is the perfect size to make bubbles." Demonstrate how well the wand in the bottle works. Instruct them to open their bubbles and play with them.

Family Discussion

Say: "Parents are like the right-sized wand. Not too little or too big. God gave you the right kind of parents that you need to raise you. Children need instruction and discipline. Too little won't work. Too much discipline can discourage a child."

What Should We Do?

1. **Ask:** "What is an example of too little instruction at home? How about at school?"
2. **Ask:** "What might happen if your coach didn't show you anything about how to play your sport?"

3. **Ask:** "What is an example of too much discipline at home?"

Adapting for . . .

Younger Children
Skip the two Discussion questions and **Say:** "God made you to be in our family because you fit. We are the right size for you and you are the right size for us. Just like your shoes fit your feet, you fit our family."

Teens
Reread the Scripture and **Ask:** "What do you think 'approved by the Lord' means?" (Discipline that is based on God's Word, the Bible; and balanced—not too little and not too much.)

Today's Slogan: "Families need balanced training."

Prayer: *Dear heavenly Father, help us be a balanced family as we train and grow together. In Jesus' name, Amen.*

THE LAST WORD

Main Point: The focus of my heart has consequences.

Materials Needed: Play costume clothes for boys and girls, CD player, recorded music, pen, and paper

Warm-up

Ask: "Have you ever had an argument and tried to get in the last word? What is the point of getting in the last word?" (To win the argument.) "Today's Scripture is *God's last word* in the Old Testament. It was followed by four hundred years of silence. Listen to what He says."

Bible Reading: Read aloud Malachi 4:5–6:

Look, I am sending you the prophet Elijah before the great and dreadful day of the Lord arrives. His preaching will turn the hearts of parents to their children, and the hearts of children to their parents. Otherwise I will come and strike the land with a curse.

What Does the Bible Say?
Ask: "What does it mean to 'turn your heart' toward some-one?" (To pay attention, care for, love and think about them, not forget about them.)

Activity: Forgetful Fashion Show

Gather some old clothes, hats, scarves, bibs, glasses, costume jewelry, aprons, and other props. **Say:** "We are going to have a fashion show. Each person gets to put on at least four but not more than seven things and parade in front of us like a fashion show for ten seconds, then leave the room. We will each try to remember what the person was wearing."

Play the catwalk music and ham it up!

Have someone record the points for each person with pen and paper. Have the model come back in after each person has tried to remember all that the model was wearing and high-light each prop. Rotate models.

Family Discussion

1. **Ask:** "What helped you remember what they were wear-ing?"
2. **Ask:** "What did not help you remember? What made it hard to remember?"
3. This game required paying attention to other members of the family. **Ask:** "What happens if we don't pay attention to each other in our family?"

Adapting for . . .

Younger Children

Emphasize that we show our caring by paying attention to each other. **Ask:** "What was I wearing yesterday?" or "What did I fix you for breakfast today?"

Teens

To deepen the Discussion, **Ask:** "Why should the parents turn their hearts to their children? Why should children turn their hearts to their parents?"

Today's Slogan: "We experience God's best when we pay attention to each other."

Prayer: *God, there are so many things that grab our attention—that capture our hearts. Help us not to be so busy or distracted that we don't connect heart-to-heart. By your grace, Amen.*

SESSION 19

HOPE RUNS FREE
(MOViE NiGHT)

Main Point: With the right focus, we won't get off course.

Materials Needed: Newspaper, blindfold, trash can, *Chariots of Fire* movie

Warm-up

Play "Blind Trashball": Wad up newspaper into balls. Use a towel or bandana as a blindfold. **Say:** "We are going to see how many of these paper balls we can get in the trash can." (Let everyone shoot.) "Now we are going to see how well we shoot when we can't see." (Blindfold volunteers.) "We have to keep our eyes on the goal if we are going to make it. If we lose sight, we will miss it."

Bible Reading: Read aloud Hebrews 12:1–2:

Do you see what this means—all these pioneers who blazed the way, all these veterans cheering us on? It means we'd better get on with it. Strip down, start running—and never quit! No extra spiritual fat, no parasitic sins. Keep your eyes on Jesus, who both began and finished this race we're in. Study how he did it. Because he never lost sight of where he was headed—that exhilarating finish in and with God. (THE MESSAGE)

What Does the Bible Say?
Ask: "Who are some heroes of the Bible that show us how to live?"

Today's Slogan: "Focus right—finish strong."

Activity: *Chariots of Fire*

If your children are under twelve, they may not stay tuned in to the entire movie, so just play the scenes where Eric has to make a decision about competing on Sunday.

Family Discussion

1. **Ask:** "How did Eric keep his focus on Jesus?" (By honoring Sunday as the Sabbath; by praying and reading the Bible.)
2. **Ask:** "What kind of pressure did he face?" (To give in; to compromise.)
3. **Ask:** "What do you admire or like about Eric Liddell?"

What Should We Do?
4. By thinking about Eric as a strong and courageous example, it can help us. **Ask:** "What are some ways we could follow Eric's example?"

Adapting for . . .

Younger Children
Select a shorter movie—one that is oriented for preschoolers. There are several *VeggieTales* videos that would work. Watch a video and **Ask** a few questions like, "How did some characters in the video learn to hang in there and not give up?" and

"Why is it good for us to keep trying when something is hard, like learning to tie your shoe?"

Teens
To deepen the Discussion, **Ask:** "What are some ways you are tempted to give in and compromise?"

Prayer: *Give us the kind of courage that Eric had, to keep our focus on you, Lord; to be courageous and willing to stand alone, so that we might finish the race. Amen.*

J O U R N A L
RECORD YOUR FAMiLY TiME MEMORiES
& EXPERiENCES HERE

LiVE LONG AND PROSPER

Main Point: We must obey the authorities God has placed in our lives.

Materials Needed: A neighborhood park

Warm-up

Ask: "Is there someone in the world who can say, 'You're not the boss of me'?" (Your child might say the president, or some strong person.) "God is the biggest boss of all. He has helpers who are our bosses or authorities. We have to do what they say. Who are some?" (Teachers, police officers, fire fighters, parents, etc.) "We have to do what these people say to keep us safe and to stay alive."

Bible Reading: Read aloud Ephesians 6:1–3:

Children, obey your parents because you belong to the Lord, for this is the right thing to do. "Honor your father and mother." This is the first of the Ten Commandments that ends with a promise. And this is the promise: If you honor your father and mother, "you will live a long life, full of blessing."

What Does the Bible Say?
Ask: "Obeying parents is the right thing to do because you (the child) belong to God. He wants us (parents) to take really good care of you. What do you think about belonging to God?"

Activity/Discussion: Park Walk

If you live near a neighborhood park, walk to it. Try to use a crosswalk and point out the lines painted on the street. When you get to the park, sit down and . . .
1. **Ask:** "Why did we use the crosswalk?" (Because it's safer. It's the law.)
2. **Ask:** "Why don't we cross wherever we want to?" (Because a car might hit us.) Most parks have rules posted. Point to the sign and **Ask:** "Why do they have rules at a park?"

What Should We Do?
3. **Ask:** "What would happen if they didn't have any rules?" (Dogs would mess up the park; equipment would be broken; cars would be parked on the playground, etc.) **Say:** "To have fun, we need rules. To live a long life, we have to follow God's rules and obey our parents. That's why, when you were little and I told you not to run into the street, you had to obey. Sometimes we don't always see the reason when we are young, but we still have to obey." (After prayer, enjoy the park.)

Adapting for . . .

Younger Children
If the park rules are posted, read the sign to your child and explain the rules. If there isn't a sign, explain some park etiquette to your child. (Example: "We take turns.")

Teens
Instead of going to a park, try out some batting cages, miniature golf, or bumper boats or cars and have fun. Adapt the Discussion questions to fit. (Example: "What would happen if you ignored the rules at the batting cages?")

Today's Slogan: "Obeying parents leads to God's best."

Prayer: *Dear heavenly Father, sometimes it's hard to obey our parents, but we know we will have your best when we do. Amen.*

J O U R N A L
RECORD YOUR FAMiLY TiME MEMORiES & EXPERiENCES HERE

THE ENDANGERED SPECiES

Main Point: Everything I need comes from following the Shepherd.

Materials Needed: Cotton balls, tape, candy, purse, bathrobe, and broomstick

Warm-up

Ask: "What would it be like to live under the freeway bridge?" (Too noisy, we could never talk; hard to sleep.) **Say:** "As a family, we need to slow down and not be too busy or too noisy to be with each other, hear each other, and relax together. Rest is almost like an endangered species."

Bible Reading: Read aloud Psalm 23:1–3:

The Lord is my shepherd; I have everything I need.
He lets me rest in green meadows; he leads me beside peaceful streams.
He renews my strength.
He guides me along right paths, bringing honor to his name.

Activity: Indoor Shepherding

Use cotton balls and tape to make each person a "sheep" except you. Tape a ball on the nose and tail of each "sheep." Use a mop or broom as your shepherd's staff. Use an old purse with a shoulder strap to hide individually wrapped candies. Wear your bathrobe or a blanket and **Say:** "I am the shepherd and my sheep follow me." The sheep should "baa" and follow you around (like Follow the Leader) on all fours. After a few minutes of following you, **Say:** "My sheep have everything they need." Guide them into another room where you have secretly hidden some of the candies beforehand. See if they can find them as they graze. **Say:** "The shepherd lets his sheep rest." Have them pretend to sleep. **Say:** "He leads them beside peaceful streams." Guide them into the bathroom and turn on the water in the bathtub. **Say:** "The shepherd renews their strength with food." Toss each sheep a candy from your purse. **Say:** "The shepherd guides his sheep away from danger and along the *right* paths." Pretend you are going to the garage or out the front door, but circle back.

Family Discussion

What Should We Do?
1. **Ask:** "Why is it important to be a good follower?"
2. **Ask:** "What makes a good shepherd?" (A leader; someone who cares about the sheep; a courageous person, etc.)
3. **Ask:** "Why do we need rest in order to enjoy each other?" (It takes time to connect.)

Today's Slogan: "God is my good shepherd. I can follow Him."

Adapting for . . .

Younger Children
The activity will probably work fine with your child, but they may not understand some of the words in the Scripture, so take time to explain them if they don't.

Teens
Your teen may be too "cool" to pretend he is a little sheep, so switch roles and have your teen be the shepherd and you and the others be the sheep. If he still won't play along, skip the Activity and lead a Discussion on who are the shepherds of today's teens—the people teens follow and have an allegiance to.

Prayer: *Dear heavenly Father, thank you that I can trust you to guide me where I'll be safe and that you provide all that I need, because you love me. I will follow you. Amen.*

REST IS A GOD IDEA

Main Point: Resting on the Sabbath is God's idea, one we should follow.

Materials Needed: Shoeboxes, construction paper, glue, old magazines, scraps of fabric, and scissors

Warm-up

Ask: "Where would be a fun place to take a nap? Where would be a really dumb place to take a nap?" **Say:** "God made us. He knows we need rest. When we don't get enough rest we get grumpy and we don't get along with each other."

Bible Reading: Read aloud Genesis 2:2–3:

On the seventh day, having finished his task, God rested from all his work. And God blessed the seventh day and declared it holy, because it was the day when he rested from his work of creation.

What Does the Bible Say?
Ask: "Why do you think God rested? Was He tired?" (No, it was more of an example for us to follow.)

Activity: Shoebox Beds

Use shoeboxes and construction paper to make miniature beds. Working in pairs, make a headboard and footboard out of construction paper. Glue scraps of fabric on the top of the lid as a bedspread and decorate the inside and outside with cutouts of magazine photos showing people resting or having fun. Each pair should copy today's Scripture on a piece of paper and glue it inside the box lid. When the beds are done, have each team share and describe their pictures. **Say:** "As we think of other ideas on how to rest, let's write them down and put them in our Shoebox Beds."

Family Discussion

What Should We Do?
1. **Ask:** "When do you feel most rested? When do you wish you could get some rest?"
2. **Ask:** "What can we do as a family to make sure we rest together at least once a week?"

Adapting for . . .

Younger Children
Assist your child with the cutting of the paper and fabric. Explain to her that our "seventh day" is the day we attend church and do things that remind us of God and how much He loves us.

Teens

Brainstorm ideas on how individual family members and the entire family can create time to rest—"margins" in life to recuperate and reconnect with each other. Select the best ideas and place them in the shoebox. Choose one to do for that week.

Today's Slogan: "A happy family is a rested family."

Prayer: *Dear heavenly Father, help us to follow your example and take time to rest. Help us to take time to worship you and make time for each other. In Jesus' name, Amen.*

J O U R N A L
RECORD YOUR FAMiLY TiME MEMORiES
& EXPERiENCES HERE

A DAY OF REST

Main Point: We should take one day a week for worship and rest.

Materials Needed: Shoelaces (or twine)

Warm-up

Ask: "What is your favorite day of the week and why?" (Have everyone respond.)

Bible Reading: Read aloud Exodus 20:8–10:

Remember to observe the Sabbath day by keeping it holy. Six days a week are set apart for your daily duties and regular work, but the seventh day is a day of rest dedicated to the Lord your God. On that day no one in your household may do any kind of work.

What Does the Bible Say?
Ask: "What do you think of when you hear the word *holy*?"

Today's Slogan: "We work together. We rest together. We worship together."

Activity: Centipede

As the family stands single-file, tie each person's shoes to the person in front of them, with the left feet tied to left feet and right feet tied to right feet. (Do not tie the left foot to the right.) The goal is to get a centipede effect, with legs moving together in motion. Slowly step together, left foot then right. Create some obstacles to go around. *Safety tip:* Have the youngest kids in front of someone who can assist in case of a fall.

Family Discussion

What Should We Do?
1. **Ask:** "What did we you learn by doing *Centipede*?" (I noticed that . . . we have to go slow and work together; we can't leave anyone out, etc.) Let kids identify their own learning, not a single correct answer.
2. **Ask:** "How did you we get around the obstacles?" (By talking and working together.)
3. **Ask:** "*Holy* means 'to set apart, be special, not like everything else.' If we set aside a day for Sabbath and make it special, we do different things on that day. What are some things that we do to remember God on our holy day?"
4. **Ask:** "If we are too busy, we miss time with God and each other. Worship and spending time together as a family are important to God. What happens if we don't make time for one another? For God?"

Adapting for . . .

Younger Children
Make the obstacles simple and the course short.

Teens
Make the course more difficult and longer. Deepen the Discussion and **Ask:** "What are some things we should stop doing in order to have more time for God and one another? What are some things we could do together on our day of rest?"

Prayer: *Dear heavenly Father, thank you for your example of taking time for worship. You deserve our praise. Thank you for your example of taking time for rest—we need it. Amen.*

J O U R N A L
RECORD YOUR FAMiLY TiME MEMORiES & EXPERiENCES HERE

ONLY ONE THiNG IS NEEDED

Main Point: Sometimes tasks can take us away from what is most important.

Materials Needed: A sturdy kitchen chair

Warm-up

Ask: "If we have company—people who visit our home—would you rather sit with our guest and listen to his stories, or would you rather help get the meal ready? Why?"

Bible Reading: Read aloud Luke 10:38–42:

As they continued their travel, Jesus entered a village. A woman by the name of Martha welcomed him and made him feel quite at home. She had a sister, Mary, who sat before the Master, hanging on every word he said. But Martha was pulled away by all she had to do in the kitchen. Later, she stepped in, interrupting them. "Master, don't you care that my sister has abandoned the kitchen to me? Tell her to lend me a hand." The Master said, "Martha, dear Martha, you're fussing far too much and getting yourself worked up over nothing. One thing only is essential, and Mary has chosen it— it's the main course, and won't be taken from her." (THE MESSAGE)

Today's Slogan: "People come before things."

Family Discussion

What Does the Bible Say?
1. **Ask:** "Do you think Mary was being lazy by not helping her sister?"
2. **Ask:** "Why didn't Jesus tell Mary to go and help Martha?"

What Should We Do?
3. **Ask:** "Some people are *Doers* while others are *Relaters*. Martha was a *Doer*—she was all about getting the task done. Mary was a *Relater*—she was interested in people and didn't pay attention to the work. Which are you?"

Activity: Chair Lift

Say: "There is a time to talk and a time for tasks, but if we work together, the task is easier AND we can talk." Have someone sit in a sturdy kitchen chair. Ask each person to try to lift the seated person and the chair. **Say:** "By yourself this task is too difficult, but let's try it together." Have the entire family lift the person and the chair a few inches off the floor. **Say:** "Many hands make the work light."

Adapting for . . .

Younger Children
Adjust the vocabulary in Discussion question 3 to "Who are you more like in the story, Martha (who was busy in the kitchen) or Mary (who sat at Jesus' feet)?"

If your children are too young to help lift a person, instead lift phone books or other books.

Teens

Develop the idea of *Doers* and *Relaters* and **Ask:** "What situations call for more of a *Doer* mentality? What situations are more suited for a *Relater?*"

Prayer: *Dear Father, help us to know when to talk and when to work. We want to be the kind of family that helps each other with difficult tasks. Thank you for the strength we have together. Amen.*

J O U R N A L
RECORD YOUR FAMiLY TiME MEMORiES & EXPERiENCES HERE

THE LUXURY OF SiTTiNG

Main Point: We need to be willing to stop, listen, and serve each other.

Materials Needed: A bucket, washcloths, towels, warm water with a little soap in it, a chair, and perfume or cologne

Warm-up

Ask: "What is your favorite smell? Would you buy a perfume of this smell?"

Bible Reading: Read aloud John 12:3:

Then Mary took a twelve-ounce jar of expensive perfume made from essence of nard, and she anointed Jesus' feet with it and wiped his feet with her hair. And the house was filled with fragrance.

Today's Slogan: "Sometimes the best gift is time."

Activity: Foot Washing

What Does the Bible Say?
Prepare a bucket with warm water and a little soap in it, wash-cloths, towels, and a chair. **Say:** "Mary did more than the usual custom of the time—washing the feet of her house-guests; she sat at Jesus' feet to listen and learn from Him. Then she took out some expensive perfume—worth a whole year's pay—and sprinkled it all over Jesus' feet. In Jesus' time they wore sandals, and their feet got dirty because they had to walk everywhere. They didn't have cars then. Today we are going to wash each other's feet." Take turns washing each other's feet. Pat them dry and then sprinkle them with some cologne or perfume.

Family Discussion

What Should We Do?
1. **Ask:** "How did it feel to have someone wash your feet?"
2. **Ask:** "Which did you like better: washing, or having your feet washed?"
3. **Ask:** "Washing feet was appreciated in Bible times because people always had dirty, tired feet from walking. Today we have other needs that still require us to serve others. Some-times it might mean that we simply stop what we are doing and listen to the other person in our family. Would this be easy or hard for you? Why?"

Adapting for . . .

Younger Children

Go through the Activity and Discussion quickly; otherwise your little ones may be tempted to play in the water. Remove the water for the Discussion.

Teens

Deepen the Discussion and **Ask:** "When Mary put perfume on Jesus' feet it was considered extravagant, even scandalous, because 'good' women weren't supposed to touch men's feet like that. Why do you think Mary took the risk to do this? What was she trying to show?"

Prayer: *Lord, help us to make time for each other and to look for ways to serve each other. In Jesus' name, Amen.*

JOURNAL
RECORD YOUR FAMiLY TiME MEMORiES & EXPERiENCES HERE

FAVORiTES
(MOViE NiGHT)

Main Point: Playing favorites is hurtful.

Materials Needed: *Toy Story* movie, popcorn, and bowls

Warm-up

Gather the family and two bowls and **Say:** "We are going to watch a movie and have popcorn, but we only have enough for two people—me (take a bowl) and someone else (hold it up). Who should it be?" After a few minutes of mayhem, choose someone, and then to the others, **Ask:** "How do you feel about this?" (Unfair, playing favorites, etc.) **Say:** "Actually, I was just trying to illustrate the point. You all will get popcorn, and your own bowls. Today we are talking about playing favorites—not being fair."

Bible Reading: Read aloud James 3:16–17:

Whenever you're trying to look better than others or get the better of others, things fall apart and everyone ends up at the others' throats. Real wisdom, God's wisdom, begins with a holy life and is characterized by getting along with others. It is gentle and reasonable, overflowing with mercy and blessings, not hot one day and cold the next, not two-faced. (THE MESSAGE)

What Does the Bible Say?
Ask: "What happens when we try to show off and look better than someone else?" (It leads to problems.)

Today's Slogan: "Being real and fair is smart."

Activity: *Toy Story*

Pop some popcorn and get comfy for a fun movie. Take a few minutes at the end to discuss the film.

Family Discussion

1. **Ask:** "Who said, 'They'll see. I'm still Andy's favorite toy'?" What happened?

What Should We Do?
2. **Ask:** "What happens when people play favorites? How did this happen in the movie?"
3. **Ask:** "What helped patch things up in the end?"
4. **Ask:** "What can we learn from this movie?"

Adapting for . . .

Younger Children
If they are tired or restless, you may want to watch the movie in two sittings.

Teens

Extend the Discussion and **Ask:** "What are some ways you see people play favorites at school? On the athletic field? With friends?"

Prayer: *Dear God, help us to be fair with our friends and family. This is the smart way to live. Amen.*

J O U R N A L
RECORD YOUR FAMiLY TiME MEMORiES & EXPERiENCES HERE

BE WiSE

Main Point: We should be content with what we have.

Materials Needed: Construction paper, tape, and markers

Warm-up

Ask: "What are some things that we as parents and kids sometimes whine or complain about?" Write these on a large piece of paper.

Bible Reading: Read aloud James 3:13–16:

If you are wise and understand God's ways, live a life of steady goodness so that only good deeds will pour forth. And if you don't brag about the good you do, then you will be truly wise! But if you are bitterly jealous and there is selfish ambition in your hearts, don't brag about being wise. This is the worst kind of lie. For jealousy and selfishness are not God's kind of wisdom. Such things are earthly, unspiritual, and motivated by the Devil. For wherever there is jealousy and selfish ambition, there you will find disorder and every kind of evil.

What Does the Bible Say?
Ask: "If you whine about what you don't have, does it make you feel better or change anything?" (No) "So how do we keep from whining? That is today's lesson."

Today's Slogan: "Contentment is a choice."

Family Discussion

1. **Ask:** "Why does wanting something that belongs to someone else cause problems?" (It leads to envy or stealing.)

What Should We Do?
2. **Ask:** "How does being selfish (not sharing) create problems?"

Activity: Prayer Chain

Using strips of construction paper, tape, and markers, make links of things you are thankful for and content with having. This is an anti-jealousy prescription. Each person should write or draw a description of at least five things, then link them together, alternating from person to person. You could also add his or her name to each link. Try to make your chain at least six feet long and display it in a prominent place in your home. Option: Have each person use a different color paper so he or she can find their own in the chain to reaffirm their thoughts.

Adapting for . . .

Younger Children
Reduce the links of contentment to three for each child.

Teens
To deepen the Discussion, **Ask:** "How does jealousy and self-ish ambition lead to disorder and evil?" Give an example using teens.

Prayer: *We are thankful to you, Lord, for the many things you have given us: our home, our health, our family. But most of all, your Son and our new life in Him. Help us to be content with all of these wonderful gifts of grace. In Jesus' name, Amen.*

J O U R N A L
RECORD YOUR FAMiLY TiME MEMORiES
& EXPERiENCES HERE

FAMiLiES WiTH PURPOSE—1

Main Point: We should do good deeds for God's approval, not people's.

Materials Needed: Groceries for a sack lunch, ingredients to make cookies, or a gift card for groceries

Warm-up

Ask: "What do you think about those kids at school who get a good grade, then parade it around, showing off? What about those football players who show off in the end zone after making a touchdown? Too much show?"

Bible Reading: Read aloud Matthew 6:1–4:

Take care! Don't do your good deeds publicly, to be admired, because then you will lose the reward from your Father in heaven. When you give a gift to someone in need, don't shout about it as the hypocrites do—blowing trumpets in the synagogues and streets to call attention to their acts of charity! I assure you, they have received all the reward they will ever get. But when you give to someone, don't tell your left hand what your right hand is doing. Give your gifts in secret, and your Father, who knows all secrets, will reward you.

What Does the Bible Say?

Ask: "Why do these fake lovers of God (hypocrites) like to show off in front of others?" (So others will be impressed with them.)

Today's Slogan: "We live for an audience of One."

Activity: Stealth Service

What Should We Do?

Think of someone in your community who is needy. They could be homeless, out of work, discouraged, sad because of a loss, or facing a life-threatening illness. To your kids, **Ask:** "What could we do to encourage and help this person?" (For example, make a sack lunch for the homeless; send a card with a grocery gift card to encourage others; bake cookies and visit someone for a short time.) Decide what to do and carry out your mission, but keep it top secret! Read today's Bible verses again.

Family Discussion

1. **Ask:** "What did you think about doing the *stealth service*?"
2. **Ask:** "What changed after we served?" (Started to think of others.)
3. **Ask:** "Why did Jesus say not to call attention to yourself when you serve?" (Because your only reward is others noticing what you've done.)

Adapting for . . .

Younger Children

Change the Warm-up question to "What's wrong with being a tattletale?" (You are trying to get someone else in trouble and make yourself look good.) You will also need to explain the slogan. Try: "God sees all that we do. We should be more concerned with what He thinks than with what people think."

Teens

Brainstorm several ways they could do service and make it "stealth." Write down the ideas and select one. The other ideas could be used later. Teens will like the stealth element of the activity. Also, to deepen the Discussion, **Ask:** "Can you imagine *tooting your own horn*—actually blowing a trumpet when you do a good deed? Why is this so obnoxious?"

Prayer: *Dear heavenly Father, help us to serve others without expecting payback or attention on us. Teach us to seek only your reward. Amen.*

FAMiLiES WiTH PURPOSE—2

Main Point: Everybody needs time to recharge.

Materials Needed: Battery-powered toy or tool, nutrition bars, and sports drinks

Warm-up

Hold up a battery-powered toy or tool. Turn it on and **Ask:** "What happens if I leave this on for a long time, like overnight?" (The battery will go dead.) **Say:** "Today we will learn that we need to recharge too when we get tired, just like this rechargeable battery."

Bible Reading: Read aloud Luke 5:15–16:

Yet despite Jesus' instructions, the report of his power spread even faster, and vast crowds came to hear him preach and to be healed of their diseases. But Jesus often withdrew to the wilderness for prayer.

What Does the Bible Say?
Ask: "Why did Jesus sometimes pull away from the crowds?" (For prayer.)

Today's Slogan: "Everybody needs to recharge."

Family Discussion

1. **Ask:** "What makes you tired or worn-out?"

What Should We Do?
2. **Ask:** "What helps you get your strength back (recharge)?" (Take a nap.)
3. **Ask:** "God told us to recharge every week by keeping the Sabbath and worshiping Him rather than working on that day. Why is this so important?" (To focus on Him; renew our relationships; rest.)
4. **Ask:** "Jesus didn't always meet the demands of the crowds. He knew He needed time alone to pray and renew His strength. How does prayer give us strength?"

Activity: Hike 'n' Snack

Get one nutrition bar and one sports drink per person. Get on comfortable walking shoes and go on a hike. Make it appropriate for the age of your youngest child. Midway, stop, sit down, and have your drink and snack. When finished, **Ask:** "Did that recharge you? Did you get more energy from the bar and the drink?" Take a few answers, then **Say:** "We need to do the same thing every week—we need to take a break for rest and worship." Then finish the hike.

Adapting for . . .

Younger Children
Ask: "What happens when you don't get a nap?" For the
Activity, keep the hike short, maybe only fifteen minutes total.

Teens
To deepen the Discussion, **Ask:** "In some of the sports you've
participated in or observed recently, how do the athletes rest
and catch their breath in the middle of the game?"

Prayer: *Thank you, God, for our bodies and rest and how you
renew us every morning. In Jesus' name, Amen.*

J O U R N A L
RECORD YOUR FAMiLY TiME MEMORiES
& EXPERiENCES HERE

FAMiLiES WiTH PURPOSE—3

Main Point: I want to advance God's kingdom, not mine.

Materials Needed: Individually wrapped candies, an ice-cream scoop, large bowl, and blindfold

Warm-up

Ask: "Why does a basketball or soccer coach have to watch the game? Why can't she hang out at the snack bar?" (Because she has to watch the game to tell the players what to do in order to play better.) **Say:** "God is like a coach—to live right, we need to listen to Him."

Bible Reading: Read aloud Matthew 6:9–11:

Our Father in heaven, may your name be honored.
May your Kingdom come soon.
May your will be done here on earth, just as it is in heaven.
Give us our food for today.

What Does the Bible Say?

Ask: "What do you think of when you think of a kingdom?"

Today's Slogan: "God's kingdom is where He rules."

Activity: Sweet Scoops

Get some individually wrapped candies (such as Hershey's kisses), an ice-cream scoop, a large plastic bowl, and a blindfold. Sit in a circle on the carpet or a rug. Randomly spread ten of the candies on the floor. Blindfold the child and **Say:** "You have thirty seconds to collect the candy, but you have to do it blindfolded and with one arm behind your back. You can only pick them up with the scoop. You get to keep the ones that get in the bowl. Go!" Have everyone else count slowly to thirty. He may only get a few in. When time's up, **Say:** "Now let's do this with help. Listen to your guide for directions." (Choose a volunteer guide.) Repeat the process, this time with the guide verbally directing the "blind" volunteer. Take turns. Share the candy.

Family Discussion

What Should We Do?

Say: "We advance God's kingdom by letting Him rule areas of our lives. We don't always know how to do this at first. We grow by turning over each area for His will to be done in it."
1. **Ask:** "What was the difference between doing it by yourself and having a guide?"
2. **Ask:** "Was it more fun with a guide?"
3. **Ask:** "God is our guide, and we need to listen to Him, even though it may not be exactly what we want—He sees things we don't see. Give me an example."

Adapting for . . .

Younger Children

Don't spread out the candy too far from them. If they have difficulty, allow them to use the hand that was behind their back to help them find the candy.

Teens

Add a couple of dollar bills crumpled up into balls. Allow them to see these before they are blindfolded. To deepen the Discussion, **Ask:** "Doing God's will may go against what a teen might want to do. Can you think of a few examples?" ("Doing what my parents say, even though I think it's dumb.")

Prayer: *Help me, God, to trust in you and let you be in charge of my life, especially when I want to be the boss. Amen.*

MAY I SERVE YOU?

Main Point: Learning to give can be fun and rewarding.

Materials Needed: Car to go to a dollar store, one dollar and one dime for each family member, pen, and paper

Warm-up

Ask everyone to describe a time when they gave a gift to someone and the person really liked it.

Bible Reading: Read aloud Acts 20:35:

And I have been a constant example of how you can help the poor by working hard. You should remember the words of the Lord Jesus: "It is more blessed to give than to receive."

What Does the Bible Say?
Ask: "Why would giving make someone happy?"

Today's Slogan: "The real joy in living is giving."

Activity: Cheap Shopping Spree

Give each person one dollar (and a dime for tax, if needed).
You will be going to a dollar store, or any store that has a
selection of one-dollar items. **Say:** "Each of us is going to buy
a secret just-for-fun gift for someone else in the family." (Draw
names for the assignments.) "Your job is to find something
that is a perfect fit for the person, or is silly, useful, or just
plain fun! You will have fifteen minutes to shop. We will meet
in front of the store in fifteen minutes and wrap the gifts at
home. Keep it a secret!"

Family Discussion

Back home, after you've opened the wrapped gifts . . .
1. **Ask:** "Did you have fun shopping?"
2. Read aloud the Scripture and **Ask:** "What does it mean to
be blessed? Why is this blessing (through giving) better than
receiving?"
3. **Ask:** "How did you feel when your person opened their
gift?"

Adapting for . . .

Younger Children
A parent or older child should accompany younger children. If
you have more than one young child, take turns buying the

gifts. You will need to help your preschooler choose a gift and wrap it at home. But remind them that it is a secret!

Teens
Extend the Discussion and **Ask:** "What are some other gifts—the kind you don't have to buy—that we can give each other in our family?" Also, ask your teen to accompany a younger sibling if needed.

Prayer: *Teach us, Father, that it is more blessed to give than to receive. Help us to see how we can do this every day. Amen.*

J O U R N A L
RECORD YOUR FAMiLY TiME MEMORiES
& EXPERiENCES HERE

SHARiNG BEGiNS WiTH HOLDiNG THiNGS LOOSELY

Main Point: All that we have can fall apart, break, or be stolen.

Materials Needed: Drawing paper, markers or crayons, a shoebox or small cardboard box, brown or black construction paper, glue, rope, bangles, and small knickknacks from around the house. Optional: thin strips of balsa wood

Warm-up

Ask: "What is your most prized possession? Your favorite thing in all the world?"

Bible Reading: Read aloud Matthew 6:19–21:

Don't store up treasures here on earth, where they can be eaten by moths and get rusty, and where thieves break in and steal. Store your treasures in heaven, where they will never become moth-eaten or rusty and where they will be safe from thieves. Wherever your treasure is, there your heart and thoughts will also be.

What Does the Bible Say?
Ask: "What is a treasure?" (Something that is worth a lot, either in money or memories. We think about our treasures; they are important to us.)

Today's Slogan: "Your treasure is what is on your heart."

Activity: Treasure Chest

Build a treasure chest out of a box with brown or black construction paper glued to the sides. (You could also use thin strips of balsa wood, glued to the box.) Decorate with knick-knacks from around the house (hardware, rope, bangles, etc.). Have each person draw two or three pictures of their favorite things: toys, clothes, food, entertainment, etc., and place these in the chest. **Say:** "We need to hide the treasure chest in a safe place; you stay here while I do that. No peeking." Hide it in a challenging but not impossible place. Then have your children look for it. If you have time, repeat the process with the finder hiding it.

Family Discussion

After you find the chest . . .

What Should We Do?
1. **Ask:** "Even though we hid our favorite treasures, they can be destroyed by rust or moths, or thieves could steal them. How would you feel if someone actually stole your favorite thing?"
2. **Ask:** "If we spend most of our time doing things that please God, we don't have so much time to pile up the things that might be lost, stolen, or damaged. God's rewards are moth-proof, rustproof, and thief-proof. What pleases God?"

3. **Ask:** "If our heart is always thinking about our stuff, it shows that our treasure is stuff. But if we are thinking about love, kindness, sharing, and being thankful, these are the treasures that last. Why are they so valuable?"

Adapting for . . .

Younger Children

This is a fairly abstract lesson, so bring the concepts down to concrete terms your child will understand. For example, **Say:** "Your treasure is your most valuable thing; it could be a toy, a doll, your favorite dress, your scooter, etc." Don't make the hiding place too high or too hard for your preschooler.

Teens

Help your teen make a break from all the materialistic hype that surrounds him or her. Extend the Discussion and **Ask:** "Do you realize that everything that you own is susceptible to being stolen, falling apart, or someone breaking it? If that's the case, what should our view be toward owning stuff?" (Hold our possessions loosely. All of our stuff really belongs to God; He's just loaned it to us.)

Prayer: *Dear heavenly Father, help us to focus our attention on you and the things of your kingdom. Help us to grow past wanting only the things of earth to wanting the true treasures. In Jesus' name, Amen.*

LOVE IS ON THE INSiDE
(MOViE NiGHT)

Main Point: True love looks beyond the looks.

Materials Needed: Popcorn, *Shrek 2* movie, old magazines, and scissors

Warm-up

Clip some pictures from magazines or newspapers of various kinds of people: strong, good-looking, happy, sad, weak, mad, etc. Hold these up, one at a time, and **Ask:** "What do you think about this person? What kind of person is she/he? What kind of mood is she/he in? Would you like this person to be your friend?"

Bible Reading: Read aloud 1 Samuel 16:7:

But the Lord said to Samuel, "Don't judge by his appearance or height, for I have rejected him. The Lord doesn't make decisions the way you do! People judge by outward appearance, but the Lord looks at a person's thoughts and intentions."

What Does the Bible Say?
Ask: "What does it mean to judge someone?" (Decide if they are good or bad by looking at their outside, not their inside.)

Today's Slogan: "Love looks deeper than the looks."

Activity: *Shrek 2*

Pop some popcorn and get comfortable for a great family movie.

Family Discussion

What Should We Do?
1. **Ask:** "How did Shrek demonstrate that true love looks beyond the looks?"
2. **Ask:** "What qualities did Shrek show that you liked (courage, loyalty, sense of humor)?"
3. **Ask:** "What are some ways we can show true love?"

Adapting for . . .

Younger Children
Try showing the movie on Saturday or Sunday afternoon or early enough in the evening so it doesn't keep your preschooler up past his bedtime. Or consider showing it in two screenings.

Teens
This is one family movie that teens will watch more than once. Extend the Discussion and **Ask:** "What romantic

themes did you see in the movie? What was unusual about
these two characters falling in love?"

Prayer: *Father God, thank you that your love is true and goes
beyond the looks. We praise you for how you loved us, even when we
weren't so lovable. Amen.*

J O U R N A L
RECORD YOUR FAMiLY TiME MEMORiES
& EXPERiENCES HERE

LiFE IS WORSHiP

Main Point: All of life is worship.

Materials Needed: Pen, paper, plastic grocery bags, a roll of clear contact paper, crayons, scissors, and stuff from nature to be collected (leaves, sticks, buds, etc.)

Warm-up

Ask: "When is a good time to pray?" (Before meals, before tests at school, before bedtime, all the time.)

Bible Reading: Read aloud Matthew 6:32–33:

Your heavenly Father already knows all your needs, and he will give you all you need from day to day if you live for him and make the Kingdom of God your primary concern.

What Does the Bible Say?
Ask: "What will God, our heavenly Father, give us?" (All of our needs, not wants.)

Today's Slogan: "Hug each moment as a gift from God."

Family Discussion

What Should We Do?
1. **Ask:** "What are some of our daily needs?" (List them.)
2. **Ask:** "How does God meet our daily needs?"
3. **Ask:** "When you look at the beauty of God's creation, what are you thankful for?" (Sky, trees, lakes, birds, etc.; list them.)

Activity: Praise Expedition

Get outside to a park or someplace that has lots of trees and natural beauty. Bring your lists of daily needs and what you are thankful for, along with a plastic grocery bag for each person. You are on an expedition to collect things that remind you of God and how He provides for you. Spend ten minutes collecting the material and then sit down at a picnic table or return home with your findings to make *Praise Mats* (place mats of praise). Using the leaves and other natural findings, along with crayon drawings illustrating how God provides, or what we like in nature, each person will make a place mat using clear contact paper. Cut the roll of contact paper into 11" x 17" pieces, place the drawings and natural objects on it, and then cover with another piece of clear contact paper. You may want to include today's Scripture verses or Slogan on the *Praise Mat*.

Adapting for . . .

Younger Children

Help your child collect the leaves and nature materials. Pre-cut the contact paper and help her place items on the sticky surface and cover with the second layer of contact paper. She may need help in writing her name or other words that she wants for her Praise Mat.

Teens

Encourage them to pick a quality of God as a theme for their Praise Mat, such as "grace" or "awesome" or "light," and find elements of nature to illustrate it. They may also draw or paint scenes for their Praise Mat, in which case you will need water-color paints or markers.

Prayer: *Dear heavenly Father, help us to see you in each part of our lives—our family, our friends, at school, in our neighborhood, and in the beautiful scenes of nature. There is so much to praise you for! Praise your name! Amen.*

BRiNGiNG IT HOME

Main Point: Passing on good values takes practice.

Materials Needed: Ten pennies per child, a muffin tin, masking tape, marker, pen, and paper. Cupcakes as a treat.

Warm-up

Ask: "If you spend the night in the garage, does that make you a car? Why not? How about if you spend the night in a fire station, does that make you a fire fighter? Why not?" (Because you have to do things on purpose, not just by accident. Like learning to ride a bike. You have to practice—not just look at it or think about it.)

Bible Reading: Read aloud 2 Corinthians 8:11:

Now you should carry this project through to completion just as enthusiastically as you began it. Give whatever you can according to what you have.

What Does the Bible Say?

Ask: "Describe a time when you finished something that was hard to finish."

Today's Slogan: "It won't happen by accident."

Activity: Kitchen Karnival

Gather ten pennies per child and a muffin tin with each cup numbered 1 to 12 with masking tape. **Say:** "Welcome to Kitchen Karnival. We are going to play a game of tossing our pennies into the muffin tin. The goal is to get the highest score. Each cup has a value, 1 to 12. We will go one at a time. You have to stand behind this line when you toss." (Make a line on the floor with masking tape.) "Before we start, let me demonstrate. Now watch carefully."

Throw ALL of your ten pennies at once toward or near the muffin tin. You aren't trying to get them in. They will laugh. **Ask:** "What's wrong with this?" (Too random; need to aim; try one at a time.) **Say:** "That's right. To be successful, we have to aim—one goal at a time." Let each child have a turn. Add up the score. **Say:** "We are all winners" and serve cupcakes to all. Give two to the actual winner.

Family Discussion

What Should We Do?

1. **Ask:** "Sometimes it's helpful to break a big project down into 'bite-sized' pieces. It's like the old joke 'How do you eat an elephant?' 'One bite at a time!' Why were we more successful at throwing one penny at a time?"
2. **Ask:** "Passing on good values and helping you to learn to be a good person takes practice. It takes repeating little things

over and over. What are some of those things?" (Brushing our teeth, being kind to each other, cleaning up our own messes, etc.)

3. **Ask:** "What is a 'habit'? Is it good or bad?" (Both) "Is it enough to *say* you are going to do something?" (No, you need to follow through and actually do it.)

Adapting for . . .

Younger Children

Make the toss line closer to the muffin tin. Try about three feet away. Help them add up the score.

Teens

Move the toss line farther away from the muffin tin. If you have teens and younger kids, make two toss lines, using the masking tape, with the kids' line about four to five feet away from the tin and the teens' at six feet away. Extend the Discussion and **Ask:** "What habits produce success for teens?" (Study habits, health habits, finishing difficult projects.)

Prayer: *Father God, help us to follow through on the things we say are important. Help us not to give up, but to keep practicing. Amen.*

A PEACEFUL FAMiLY

Main Point: Stress is feeling out of control. Peace is realizing God is in control.

Materials Needed: Two small Ziploc-type plastic bags, a clothes hanger (a pants hanger with clips works best), masking tape, pen, and fifty pennies

Warm-up

Ask: "When have you been stressed or worried?"

Bible Reading: Read aloud John 14:27:

I am leaving you with a gift—peace of mind and heart. And the peace I give isn't like the peace the world gives. So don't be troubled or afraid.

What Does the Bible Say?
Ask: "Where does peace come from?" (Jesus)

Today's Slogan: "I can have peace because I know God is in control."

Activity: Peace Hangs in the Balance

Gather the materials and label the plastic bags with masking tape: "Stress & Worry" on one, and "God's Control/Truth" on the other. Place a penny in each bag and clip the bags on the bottom of the pants hanger with each bag balancing the other. (If you don't have a pants hanger, use clothes pins or tape to hang the bags from a regular hanger.) "Hang" the clothes hanger over a few fingers of a volunteer.
1. **Say:** "Write something you are worried about on masking tape, using a word, abbreviation, or even a drawing, and stick it on or around a penny and then place it in the *Worry* bag."
2. **Say:** "Try to think of a truth you know about God and how He is in control. Also write it on tape and stick it to a penny, but put it in the *Truth* bag."
3. Have each person try to do three or more worries and three or more truths. **Say:** "Peace is balancing our stress and worries with God's truth and remembering that He is in control of the details of our life."

Family Discussion

What Should We Do?
1. **Ask:** "Do all people worry?" (Yes, even adults.)
2. **Say:** "Why is personal peace important?" (Because without it, we get stressed out.)
3. **Say:** "Why do we need peace in our family?" (So we can relax together and deal with worries.)

Adapting for . . .

Younger Children

You will need to help them symbolize their worries and list for them some of God's truths (God is loving, God is everywhere, God knows all things, etc.) and help them illustrate the quality about God, or write the word for them.

Teens

Extend the Discussion and **Ask:** "How can remembering that God is in control even of the details of your life bring peace?" If there are too many worries, the bag may fall from the hanger. Try using tape to hold it on. **Ask:** "What can we do to discover and remember truths about God?" (To balance the fears and worries?) (Read God's Word; attend Bible studies; worship; listen to music that focuses on God; journal; pray; be in community with other followers of Christ.)

Prayer: *Father God, help us to experience your peace—the kind that is greater than our understanding; peace that calms our worried hearts. In Jesus' name, Amen.*

A TRUTHFUL FAMiLY

Main Point: Healthy families are truthful.

Materials Needed: Twine or yarn, chair, and scissors

Warm-up

Ask: "For relationships to be healthy and strong, they have to be based on truth. People have problems when they believe things that are not true. Can you think of some fairy tales in which people believed things that weren't true? What problems did they cause?" (e.g., *The Emperor's New Clothes*—he paraded naked! In *Cinderella*, she believed she was worthless because her wicked stepmother told her she was.)

Bible Reading: Read aloud Ephesians 4:15:

Instead, speaking the truth in love, we will in all things grow up into him who is the Head, that is, Christ. (NIV)

What Does the Bible Say?

Ask: "We are to tell the truth because it is right and the loving thing to do. How would you feel if someone lied about you?" (Not loved.)

Today's Slogan: "We will balance the truth with love."

Activity: Web of Lies

Explain that when we lie it's like being caught in a spider web; it becomes more and more complex and can restrict us. Have a volunteer sit in a simple, straight chair. Secretly whisper to the volunteer, "This is one time when we want you to lie about everything. We are going to take turns asking you questions, and each time you should lie." Have the other children ask him questions: "How old are you?" or "Where do you live?" etc. After each lie, wrap more twine around him and the chair. Do not cut the twine until the end. (Don't make it so tight that you cut off circulation. Have scissors handy to cut the twine.) After he is caught in a huge web, explain to the others that you asked him to lie, and that lying gets us into a web of deceit that traps like a spider web. Go on to Discussion.

Family Discussion

What Should We Do?

1. **Ask:** "What did you think about the game *Web of Lies*?"
2. To the volunteer "liar," **Ask:** "How did it feel to lie?"
3. To everyone, **Ask:** "What would happen to our family if we really did tell that many lies?"

(After the Discussion, be sure to untie the "liar"!)

Adapting for . . .

Younger Children

You may have to explain a fairy tale or two to your child. She may not immediately get the connection between fantasy and real life.

Teens

Deepen the Discussion and explain that myths are beliefs that we hold that are familiar but not 100-percent accurate. They *seem* true, but in reality they are not. They are a common form of deception. **Ask:** "What frees us from myths and deceptions?" (Truth) Ask for examples of things we know are solid truth. For each one shared, cut away at the string of deception around the volunteer. **Say:** "Truth leads to freedom."

Prayer: *Thank you, God, that you are the true God and that there is nothing dishonest about you. We can trust you because you are truth. Because of your truth, we are free. Amen.*

Rx FOR A GOOD ATTiTUDE

Main Point: An attitude of gratitude is powerful.

Materials Needed: Empty cans, two colors of construction paper, markers, scissors, wrapping paper, and tape. *Note:* Remove lids of cans completely with an opener that smoothes sharp edges.

Warm-up

Ask: "Why does a positive attitude give you strength, but a grumpy mood makes you feel worn out?"

Bible Readings: Read aloud Proverbs 17:22:

A cheerful heart is good medicine, but a broken spirit saps a person's strength.

Read aloud Philippians 4:13:

I can do everything with the help of Christ who gives me the strength I need.

What Does the Bible Say?
Ask: "How can laughing and a cheerful heart be like medicine?" (It makes you feel better.)

Today's Slogan: "A can-do attitude brings joy."

Family Discussion

1. **Ask:** "When did someone cheer you up and make you feel better?"
2. **Ask:** "What happens if someone has a grumpy attitude?" (It rubs off on others.)
3. **Ask:** "Where could you use some extra strength this week?"

Activity: Can-Do Cans

Gather some empty fruit or vegetable cans—ideally one can per person—and the other materials. **Say:** "We are going to make reminders of what we are grateful for—things to remember that we already have. Using one color of construction paper, you can cut them out in shapes or draw them and then place them in this can, which you can decorate with wrapping paper. On the other color of construction paper, draw or cut out two or three objects to represent things we need strength for (a test at school, stress at work, making the team, etc.). On the backs of these, we will write today's Scripture verses. These will be prominently displayed as our Can-Do Cans!"

Adapting for . . .

Younger Children

Assist your child in thinking of things to display on the can and helping her cut out and illustrate her idea. She will need help in determining areas in which she could use more strength. For preschool children, it could be things like climbing the jungle gym, riding their tricycle, not being afraid at swimming lessons, and other physically challenging situations.

Teens

Deepen the Discussion and **Ask:** "Now that we have our Can-Do Cans, where should we put them to help us remember what's inside? Is there some way we can use these on a regular basis to keep us from being discouraged and grumpy?" (Collect ideas on how you might use the cans in your family.)

Prayer: Thank you, Mighty God, that because of you we can have a can-do attitude and be encouraging to others. Amen.

HEROES AT HOME
(MOViE NiGHT)

Main Point: We can be powerful when we stick together.

Materials Needed: *The Incredibles* movie and popcorn

Warm-up

Ask: "What can we do together that you can't do alone?"

Bible Reading: Read aloud Joshua 1:7:

Be strong and very courageous. Obey all the laws Moses gave you. Do not turn away from them, and you will be successful in everything you do.

What Does the Bible Say?
Ask: "What do you think about the promise 'You will be successful in everything you do'?"

Today's Slogan: "Hope makes us heroes at home."

Activity: *The Incredibles*

Pop some popcorn and enjoy the movie. Save time for Discussion afterward.

Family Discussion

1. **Ask:** "How were the Parrs different from our family?" (They have superpowers.)
2. **Ask:** "Violet and Dash wanted to fit in and be normal at the beginning of the movie, but toward the end, while they were riding in the limo, Dash says, 'I love our family.' What changed their minds?" (Discovering how to use their superpowers for good, discovering a family mission, working together.)

What Should We Do?
3. **Ask:** "What could we have as *our* family mission statement?"

Adapting for . . .

Younger Children
View the movie early enough in the day so you won't have sleepyheads at the end, or show it in two sittings. If you have a children's picture storybook Bible, show pictures from some of the Old Testament stories (like Joshua) where people of God had to be strong and courageous (David and Goliath, Daniel and the lion's den, etc.).

Teens

If your teen doesn't want to watch the entire movie, select ten minutes and watch that together, then extend the Discussion and **Ask:** "What are some ways teens need to be strong?" (Refer back to the Scripture.) "What are some ways teens can show they are courageous?"

Prayer: *Thank you, God, for our family. Thank you that we can work together and challenge evil and stand for what is good like the family did in the movie. Help us to stand together, even though it looks like the world is falling apart. In Jesus' name, Amen.*

J O U R N A L
RECORD YOUR FAMiLY TiME MEMORiES
& EXPERiENCES HERE

A HEALTHY FAMiLY STRENGTHENS CORE VALUES

Main Point: We need to be clear and consistent about what's important.

Materials Needed: Paper, pen, construction paper, poster board, markers, scissors, tape, and glue. Optional: leather, canvas, wood, or ceramic clay.

Warm-up

Ask: "What is one rule that is really important in our family? Are we consistent with it? Why or why not? What might happen if this rule were only followed on Monday, Wednesday, and Friday?"

Bible Reading: Read aloud Psalm 78:5–7:

For he issued his decree to Jacob; he gave his law to Israel. He commanded our ancestors to teach them to their children, so the next generation might know them—even the children not yet born— that they in turn might teach their children. So each generation can set its hope anew on God, remembering his glorious miracles and obeying his commands.

What Does the Bible Say?
Ask: "What will you teach your grandchildren?"

Today's Slogan: "We want to pass along God's best."

Family Discussion

What Should We Do?
1. **Ask:** "What is one thing that has been passed along from Grandma or Grandpa and is being passed along to the kids in this family?" (An appreciation for hard work; a love for home-made peach ice cream, etc.)
2. **Ask:** "What does the Bible passage say should be passed along from one generation to the next?" (Stories of God's miracles and His commands.)
3. **Ask:** "What happens if parents forget, or get too busy, to pass on their faith and love for God to their kids?" (The kids forget and stop following God.)

Activity: Family Crest Project

Make a family shield or crest based on today's Scripture. (If you already have a family Scripture, incorporate it.) Divide the crest into four parts to reflect your family's top four values (example: Love, Working Together, Honor, Justice, etc.). Make the crest out of paper, leather, wood, or ceramics. You might integrate some of the themes and experiences from past Family Times. If you have time, develop a Family Mission Statement that incorporates your top values. You may choose to display your mission statement on your crest. Display your Family Crest in a prominent place to remind family members of your *Family Mission.*

Adapting for . . .

Younger Children

Shorten the Discussion and **Ask:** "What is your favorite thing to do with Mom or Dad?" (If you can, make plans to do it as part of your Family Time or immediately afterward.) This illustrates the principle of taking the time for what matters most. Chances are it will be things like "pushing me in the swing" or "playing with me and my toys," so it won't take a huge amount of time.

Teens

Enlist teens in writing your Family Mission Statement, using the skills they have picked up from school. Try to keep it short, make it comprehensive and timeless, and make it memorable. Also, during the Discussion, **Ask:** "How can telling stories about what God has done give hope to kids and teens?"

Prayer: *Thank you, God, that you have given us a purpose as a family to be [review your values]. By your grace and strength, we will be this kind of family. In Jesus' name, Amen.*

PART TWO

SPECiAL OCCASiONS & HOLiDAYS

BACK TO SCHOOL

Main Point: We should celebrate the joy of learning.

Materials Needed: Family car or transportation and time needed to visit a museum

Warm-up

Ask: "What makes a person knowledgeable?" Answer: (He keeps on learning; he's teachable.) **Ask:** "Let's say we are on a family car trip and we get lost. What should we do?" (Stop and ask for directions from someone who lives there and knows their way around.)

Bible Reading: Read aloud Proverbs 10:17:

The road to life is a disciplined life; ignore correction and you're lost for good. (THE MESSAGE)

What Does the Bible Say?
Ask: "How is life like a road?"

Activity: Visit a Museum

Focus on the joy of learning. Prepare your children to return to school by getting excited about what others have discovered, invented, or created (arts, cars, music, technology, etc.). This outing will take longer than the usual twenty minutes, but it will give you a nice break from the hubbub of shopping for back-to-school stuff, and it focuses on the real purpose of school: learning.

If you don't have a museum nearby, watch an educational show on PBS, the Discovery Channel, or the Travel Channel. Adapt the Discussion questions accordingly.

Family Discussion

Consider packing a picnic lunch to eat at the museum. Many museums provide eating areas. During lunch . . .

1. **Ask:** "What was the most impressive thing you saw?"
2. **Ask:** "What showed a lot of discipline and hard work by the person who made the exhibit or art?"

What Should We Do?
3. **Ask:** "What are some ways we can continue being lifelong learners?" (Go to church, read the Bible, read books, visit museums, etc.)

Today's Slogan: "Wise people are lifelong learners."

Adapting for . . .

Younger Children
Keep the museum visit short, probably around one hour, and look for museums with activities and interactive exhibits for kids. Try a children's museum first.

Teens
Make a list of three or more museums and let them select the one for the family to go to. It might be dedicated to cars or fashion, but go with it. Extend the Discussion and **Ask:** "Why does discovery and creation bring joy?" and "A fool is a person who thinks he knows it all and has lost the joy of discovery. How can we keep from being foolish and retain our joy of learning?"

Prayer: *Creator God, thank you for your beautiful world that you have made for us to enjoy. The blue skies, the sparkly stars, and the powerful ocean are simply small pieces of your artistry. Help us always to be joyful about learning as an expression of our gratefulness to you. In Jesus' name, Amen.*

HALLOWEEN/HARVEST SEASON (MOViE NiGHT)

Main Point: Instead of fear and scare tactics, emphasize courage.

Materials Needed: An extreme sports video where people need courage (rock climbing, surfing, skateboarding, BMX [bicycle motocross], skydiving, or wakeboarding)

Warm-up

Ask: "What extreme sport would you like to try that requires courage?"

Bible Reading: Read aloud 2 Timothy 1:7:

For God has not given us a spirit of fear and timidity, but of power, love, and self-discipline.

What Does the Bible Say?

Ask: "Talk about a time when God gave you courage when you were afraid."

Activity: An extreme sports movie

Check out videos like *The Moment of Truth,* a video that features BMX, snowboarding, surfing, and skateboarding action along with hot Christian bands.

Family Discussion

1. **Ask:** "What is courage?"
2. **Ask:** "How did the people in the video show courage?"

What Should We Do?

3. **Ask:** "How does God help us when we are afraid and need courage?"

Today's Slogan: "With God, I don't have to be afraid."

Adapting for . . .

Younger Children
Don't watch the entire movie. Watch a few action scenes and then discuss.

Teens
Select a video that teens might enjoy, like *Extreme Days,* which follows a road trip of four guys and a girl who journey to

Mexico to surf, Mammoth to snowboard, and Pismo Dunes to motocross.

Prayer: *Most Powerful God, you have the universe in your palm. Nothing happens without your knowing about it. Help us to place our trust in you and not be afraid. Amen.*

J O U R N A L
RECORD YOUR FAMiLY TiME MEMORiES & EXPERiENCES HERE

THANKSGiViNG

Main Point: We thank God, for He is good.

Materials Needed: Copies of the responsive Bible reading (one per person), wooden yardstick, construction paper, key ring, scissors, string, markers, tape or glue, and a drill

Warm-up

Ask: "This Thanksgiving, we have much to be thankful for. Name one or two things that you are thankful for."

Bible Reading: Psalm 136:1–5, 25
     Read this responsively with one person reading the first line and the rest of the family reading the *italicized* line.

Give thanks to the Lord, for he is good!
His faithful love endures forever.
Give thanks to the God of gods.
His faithful love endures forever.
Give thanks to the Lord of lords.
His faithful love endures forever.
Give thanks to him who alone does mighty miracles.
His faithful love endures forever.
Give thanks to him who made the heavens so skillfully.
His faithful love endures forever.
He gives food to every living thing.
His faithful love endures forever.

What Does the Bible Say?

Ask: "Why should we be thankful (grateful) to God?"

Activity: Yardstick Mobile of Thanks

Drill a hole at each end of a wooden yardstick—one inch from the end. Thread six feet of string through one end and tie it off. Thread the other end of the string through the center of a key ring and tie it off at the other end of the yardstick. This will create a basic mobile. You can tie another string to the key ring to hang your mobile. (All of this can be done in advance to save time during Family Time.) Gather the family and **Say:** "We are going to create a mobile of thanks—to remind us that 'God is good, all the time.' We will display this at Thanksgiving. We have thirty-six inches on the yardstick, so we need thirty-six things that we are grateful for. We have four family members, so we can each try to do about eight or nine *thanks hangings* out of construction paper. You can make them with words or symbols, or both, and we will hang them at one-inch spans." Option: Have the parents take the first eight as a timeline for the early years: how we met, where we fell in love, our wedding, our first home, the first child, etc.

Family Discussion

What Should We Do?

1. Beginning with the hanging at inch 1, **Ask** someone to describe what they created as a *Thanks Hanging* and why.
2. After you have talked about each one, **Say:** "Obviously, we have much to be thankful for in this family—past, present, and future. How should we use our mobile for Thanksgiving? Where should we display it?"

Today's Slogan: "God is good—all the time."

Adapting for . . .

Younger Children

Help them with the cutting and gluing. You may have to ask, "What are you thankful for?" and help them think of ways to illustrate it.

Teens

You can provide more sophisticated supplies, such as borders, photos, clippings from magazines, and fancy trims and graphics that you can purchase at an art or scrapbook store. You can also suggest that each inch represents a year, beginning when Dad and Mom first met. This would project into the future things like "making the team; getting to drive; graduating from high school; being accepted to a college, etc." This is thankfulness in the future—a form of grace and hope.

Prayer: *We are thankful for your goodness to us, Father, as seen with all of these blessings on our mobile. Help us to remember that your faithful love endures forever. Amen.*

CHRiSTMAS ADVENT

Main Point: Prepare your family for a Christ-centered Christmas.

Materials Needed: A large basket or cardboard box, paper, and pen

Warm-up

In early December, gather your family and **Say:** "We are going to focus on Jesus this Christmas and also other people with the theme of *giving* rather than *getting*. Don't worry, we'll still have presents, we are just going to learn how not to get overwhelmed with Christmastime stuff and busyness. What are some ways we can put Jesus first? What are some ways we can put others first?" (Record these in writing.) **Say:** "When we put others first, however we do it, we are giving them a gift."

Bible Reading: Read aloud Acts 20:35:

And I have been a constant example of how you can help the poor by working hard. You should remember the words of the Lord Jesus: "It is more blessed to give than to receive."

What Does the Bible Say?
Ask, "All the giving at Christmas can remind us of Christ's gift at that first Christmas. What is your favorite decoration that reminds us of Jesus' birth?" (Nativity scene, etc.)

Activity: Christmas Basket

Part of this lesson will impact your family grocery shopping. Once a week in December, have a *Soup Night*. Instead of a more expensive meal, you will have soup, and with the money you save, buy groceries to put into your *Christmas Basket*. Place the basket in a visible place and fill it with canned foods, candy canes, baked goods, and other festive food items. You can decorate your basket with Christmas colors, ribbons, etc. As Christmas draws closer, ask family members to pray about and look for a particular family in financial need that would benefit from your Christmas basket. Depending on the relationship, you may want to visit as a family when you drop off the basket, or simply leave it at the family's front door as a surprise.

Family Discussion

What Should We Do?
Each Soup Night, **Ask:** "How does it make you feel to give up a full meal for soup? The basket is getting more and more stuff in it as Christmas gets closer. How does that make you feel? Have your friends noticed the basket? What did they say?"

Today's Slogan: "It is more blessed to give than to receive."

Adapting for . . .

Younger Children

Involve them in decorating the basket and explaining to them how God uses us to meet the needs of others. You might consider adding a family-friendly movie to your Christmas basket for the whole family to enjoy. **Ask:** "What do you think the kids will do when they see this movie in the basket?"

Teens

Develop a Christmas Activity Plan to help pace your family in the busy holiday season. **Say:** "We want to plan a Christmas that is Christ-centered, relaxing, and fun. We can't do everything. What would you say are the most important things to do?" Develop a plan that reflects your values. Discuss the plan at the next Family Night. For example, your teen might want to skip caroling this Christmas and as a family help at a charity.

Prayer: *Father God, you gave your Son. We celebrate the birth of Jesus now. We are so grateful to you for being generous and giving us a gift that really fits—life forever with you. Thank you in Jesus' name. Amen.*

CHRiSTMAS

Main Point: Christmas is about being close. God wanted us to be close to Him, so He sent His very best—Jesus.

Materials Needed: Candle, match, shoebox, wrapping paper, ribbon, and Christmas cards from friends and family. Optional: birthday cake and candles.

Warm-up

Say: "Christmas is about being together. We can't be with everyone we love. We send Christmas cards to remember and care about others. God's Christmas *card* was Jesus. What are some ways Jesus is like a Christmas card?" (He brings good news, He expresses love, He wants to be with us, etc.)

Bible Reading: Read aloud John 8:12:

Jesus said to the people, "I am the light of the world. If you follow me you won't be stumbling through the darkness, because you will have the light that leads to life."

Activity: Prayer Box

Decorate a *Christmas Card Prayer Box* (see suggestion for Younger Children) and place it on your kitchen table. On December 12 or 13, and every day until Christmas, choose one of the Christmas cards that you have received and place it vertically in the *Christmas Card Prayer Box*. Before meals, take out a card from the front of the box and pray for that family as you thank God for your food. Then, place the card at the back of the box. You may want to remember something specific that is mentioned in the card or letter. Example: "God, thank you for the Robinsons. We pray for the dad, who is recovering from being in the hospital. Heal him, and give them a joyful Christmas. Thanks for this food. Amen."

Variation: You may select twelve families and make your own card that represents each by using their family photo or an index card with their names, ages, and address on it.

Family Discussion

What Should We Do?

1. After you pray for the family represented by their card, **Ask:** "What do you know about this family? Do you remember the last time we saw them?" Add other similar questions.

2. On December 24 or 25, celebrate that Jesus has come by reading, as a family, the following script:

> PARENT: Jesus has come! He is our Savior of hope, the Shepherd of peace, God's gift of love, and the baby that brings the world joy.
>
> CHILD: (Lights the candle) Why do we light this candle tonight?
>
> PARENT: Because Jesus is the Light of the World, who brings light and joy into the darkness.
>
> CHILD: Why is Jesus different?

PARENT: Because He is King of Kings and Lord of Lords, forever and ever.

CHILD: Jesus is Lord.

PARENT: We don't have to stumble in the dark. Jesus leads
the way, because . . .

ALL: Jesus is the light of the world! Happy Birthday, Jesus!

3. Conclude by talking about birthdays, Christmas, and other
celebrations that use candles and light as part of the festivities.

Option: You may choose to serve a "Happy Birthday, Jesus"
birthday cake with candles at the end of your Family Time.

Today's Slogan: "Jesus is the Light of the world."

Adapting for . . .

Younger Children

Have the youngest child in the family make the *Christmas
Card Prayer Box* with wrapping paper and ribbon wrapped
around a shoebox. You may need to help with the cutting and
gluing, but leave as much of it as possible to her. You may
want to cut a hole in the top or remove the top.

Teens

Ask: "What are some ways spiritually lost people stumble?
How can we be a light to them?"

Prayer: *Dear Father God, thank you for sending your precious Son
to be our sacrifice. We know you did this because you love us. You
want us to be together, to be close. Help us to love and know you
more this Christmas. In Jesus' name, Amen.*

NEW YEAR'S EVE

Main Point: God has provided for our needs and has given us a whole new year to appreciate what He does for us.

Materials Needed: Food for a meal, candles, sparkling cider, plastic champagne glasses, dessert, gold ribbons, silver seal stickers, and parchment-looking paper. See the *Advance Preparation* section that follows.

Warm-up

Have a nice family dinner with candlelight. At the meal, read the Scripture verses and **Ask:** "What are some ways we saw God work this past year? We don't want to forget these blessings. How can we be sure to remember them?"

Bible Reading: Read aloud Deuteronomy 8:10–14:

After a meal, satisfied, bless God, your God, for the good land he has given you. Make sure you don't forget God, your God, by not keeping his commandments, his rules and regulations that I command you today. Make sure that when you eat and are satisfied, build pleasant houses and settle in, see your herds and flocks flourish and more and more money come in, watch your standard of living going up and up—make sure you don't become so full of yourself and your things that you forget God, your God. (THE MESSAGE)

Advance Preparation: You will need to prepare a certificate for each child that commemorates *significant achievements or displays of character this past year.* You might even want to use a computer to personalize each one, including the child's name in fancy font and printed on parchment-looking paper. (Examples of achievement or character: "Learned to Read," "Made a Great Friend," "Mastered the Fine Art of Bike Riding," "Showed Compassion to Others," "Made the Varsity Team.") You can also add gold ribbons and silver seal stickers to make it look official. (Available at office supply stores.)

Activity: New Year's Eve Family Party

Set the clocks way ahead and get ready to celebrate with the kids as the clock strikes "midnight." Option: Serve chilled sparkling apple juice or cider in plastic champagne glasses and make a toast to each child as you present their certificates.

Family Discussion

What Does the Bible Say?
1. **Ask:** "What does the Bible passage say no one should forget, even when things are going great?"
2. **Ask:** "What do you think about your certificates?"
3. **Ask:** "As you look at the New Year—full of possibilities, accomplishments, and growth—what are you excited about? What do you hope for? What do you think will happen?"

Today's Slogan: "God has given us the gifts of time and each other."

Adapting for . . .

Younger Children

Set the clocks so it will be "midnight" at 7 or 8 P.M. and make an icon or a picture that illustrates your child's accomplishment on her certificate. You could also add an actual photo of her demonstrating her accomplishment (example, riding her bike).

Teens

Your teen may say something about the certificate being "cheesy," but she will keep it as proof that her parents love her and have acknowledged her growth. If you can, try to focus more on personal growth than on academic or athletic achievement.

Prayer: Dear Father God, we thank you for time—for the privilege of seeing all that you did this past year. We look forward to the future with this brand-new year where we can be alert to see you at work. We give you this day, our lives, and the year before us. Amen.

VALENTiNE'S DAY

Main Point: We learn about love and faithfulness at home.

Materials Needed: Red or white wrapping paper, cardboard box with a lid, about five or six yards of ribbon (depending on size of family), a small wrapped gift for each family member, red or white construction paper, markers, and tape. See the *Advance Preparation* section that follows.

Warm-up

Cut 2- to 3-inch hearts out of the construction paper, and with markers write something complimentary about each person: "I love this about [name]." Make sure everyone has at least two or three Love Hearts. You might put these out a day ahead of time so everyone can begin early.

Bible Reading: Read aloud John 15:13–15:

And here is how to measure it—the greatest love is shown when people lay down their lives for their friends. You are my friends if you obey me. I no longer call you servants, because a master doesn't confide in his servants. Now you are my friends, since I have told you everything the Father told me.

Advance Preparation: Purchase the gifts and wrap them (with the box and lid wrapped separately, so the lid can be easily removed). Tie a ribbon to each gift and run the ribbon to each place setting. Place the ribbon under the plate. Replace the lid. Cover the lid with love hearts (see Warm-up).

Activity: Valentine's Meal

Serve a meal that is related to Valentines: heart-shaped waffles or pancakes, cherry juice, strawberries; or bake cookies and use a heart-shaped cookie cutter. At the end of the meal, remove the lid to the box, and instruct each person (one at a time) to gently pull their ribbon and obtain their gift.

Family Discussion

What Should We Do?
1. **Ask:** "What does the Bible say about the greatest kind of love?" (Be a servant.)
2. **Ask:** "How can you be a servant to your family? At school? On the team?"

Today's Slogan: "Love is learned at home."

Adapting for . . .

Younger Children
Assist her in writing or describing her Love Heart. She may need help in drawing what she loves. Or she can tell you and you can write it. Or you can write it on a piece of paper and she can copy and color to make it pretty. Help define and illustrate love and faithfulness to your child.

Teens

Consider making the gift a nice surprise—a watch, their favorite CD, a coupon for the movies, or their favorite snack. To extend the Discussion, **Ask:** "What is the difference between friends and servants?" (The relationship between friends is one of love, not authority. "What do true friends talk about?" (Everything)

Prayer: *Dear heavenly Father, help us to learn how to love and be faithful at home, with each other, so that others might see your love in us. Amen.*

J O U R N A L
RECORD YOUR FAMiLY TiME MEMORiES
& EXPERiENCES HERE

PALM SUNDAY

Main Point: We celebrate Jesus, God's Son.

Materials Needed: Small clay pots, potting soil, a pony pack of flowers (multiple connected plastic packs of flower plants), trowel, acrylic paints and brushes, purple ribbon, orange juice, 7Up, juice glasses, and cut flowers or palm leaves

Warm-up

Ask: "Have you seen award shows where the celebrities arrive in fancy limousines and step out onto the red carpet wearing their finest clothes and jewelry? What is the purpose of the carpet and all of the attention?" (To show honor and value to someone who is important or famous.) "If a famous person visited our home, what would you do to make her or him feel welcome?"

Bible Reading: Read aloud Matthew 21:8–9 (at breakfast):

Most of the crowd spread their coats on the road ahead of Jesus, and others cut branches from the trees and spread them on the road. He was in the center of the procession, and the crowds all around him were shouting, "Praise God for the Son of David! Bless the one who comes in the name of the Lord! Praise God in highest heaven!"

What Does the Bible Say?
Ask: "Why would people spread their coats and palm branches out?" (Because they wanted to honor Jesus and they didn't have red carpet in those days.)

Activity: Palm Parade and Plantings

If you live in an area where you can get palm fronds (available at many florist shops), get at least one per family member. Rinse them outside and allow them to dry before bringing into the house. If palms aren't available, get a large bouquet of affordable cut flowers. Early on the Saturday before Palm Sunday, or on Palm Sunday, lay out the palms (or flowers) down the hall or into the kitchen. (With flowers, you will line a pathway to walk.) For your Palm Sunday celebration, make *Praise Mimosa* out of orange juice and 7Up. After breakfast, line everyone up to march and repeat, "Bless the one who comes in the name of the Lord!"

Family Discussion

1. **Ask:** "Why did Jesus show up on a donkey instead of a fancy horse?" (He came to help people, not draw attention to himself.)
2. **Ask:** "Why didn't Jesus get the *red carpet treatment* when He made His arrival into Jerusalem?" (Red carpet was not available at that time.)
3. **Ask:** "Why did the people wave palms at Jesus as He rode in on the donkey?" (It was a way of showing honor and importance to someone; usually reserved for royalty. In a way, they were calling him a "prince" by calling him "Son of King David.")
4. **Ask:** "How do we show honor and respect to Jesus now?" (By putting Him first in our lives; by thinking *what would Jesus do* in a certain situation.)

Today's Slogan: "Hallelujah! Jesus is Lord!"

Adapting for . . .

Younger Children
Preschool kids will love the marching, especially if you can add some of their music that they can march to.

Teens
Teens won't be into the marching, and they will check to make sure the drapes are closed! So let them be cool and give them palm branches to wave up and down over their younger siblings. Make the parade shorter if you have older children and teens, or skip it all together and **Ask:** "What did you think about waking up to flowers and palm leaves on the floor?" (Expect, "I thought Mom had gone crazy.")

Let teens and older children make praise plantings out of the small clay pots by decorating them with art and slogans from today's Scripture. (Example: "Bless the one who comes in the name of the Lord!") Use acrylic paints (or markers) for the decoration. When complete, place potting soil and one small flower from the pony pack in the pot. Clean off dirt and wrap with purple ribbon (representing the royalty of Jesus), then place one in each bedroom as a reminder to think of Jesus' sacrifice during the Easter season.

Prayer: *Dear Jesus, you deserve our praise. You are our Savior, God's Son, the Prince of Peace, the Everlasting One. You alone are worthy of our worship. We celebrate you! Amen.*

EASTER

Main Point: Jesus still does miracles.

Materials Needed: Large river rocks (softball to football size; one per person) and markers

---

Warm-up

Say: "Today we will celebrate Jesus' victory over death. Because He is God's Son, He had power over death. The early Christians had a saying that they said in unison. Please repeat it after me, then let's say it together twice: 'Christ has died.' (Repeat) 'Christ is risen.' (Repeat) 'Christ will come again.' (Repeat).

Bible Reading: Read aloud Matthew 28:1–7:

Early on Sunday morning, as the new day was dawning, Mary Magdalene and the other Mary went out to see the tomb. Suddenly there was a great earthquake, because an angel of the Lord came down from heaven and rolled aside the stone and sat on it. His face shone like lightning, and his clothing was as white as snow. The guards shook with fear when they saw him, and they fell into a dead faint. Then the angel spoke to the women, "Don't be afraid!" he said. "I know you are looking for Jesus, who was crucified. He isn't here! He has been raised from the dead, just as he said would happen. Come, see where his body was lying. And now, go quickly and tell his disciples he has been raised from the dead."

Activity: Rock 'n' Roll

Say: "Flowers, Easter eggs, bunnies, new clothes, baskets of candy, and pastel colors are all part of Easter, but what about rocks? A huge rock was part of the very first Easter—the one the angel *rolled* away from the grave. So let's have a *rock 'n' roll* Easter! We are going to make rocks that remind us of the resurrection miracle."

Ask: "What were some of the miracles that Jesus did?"

Say: "We will now capture those miracle stories on rocks." Have everyone take a river rock and decorate it with the markers—put symbols of God's power that help you remember stories in the Bible where the Lord did miracles. Also write in large lettering a phrase from today's Scripture, or something related to the resurrection, such as, "Don't be afraid! He isn't here. He is risen!"

Family Discussion

What Does the Bible Say?
1. **Ask:** "Why did God send the angel to roll the rock away?" (To let people see that Jesus had risen.)

What Should We Do?
2. **Ask:** "Just like God rolled the rock away, He wants to help us remove everything that keeps us from being with Jesus. What are some things that get in the way of our being with Jesus?" (Too busy; not praying; forgetting to read the Bible; not thinking about Jesus when we are worshiping at church.)

Today's Slogans: Responsive—"Christ is risen!" "He has risen indeed!" or "Jesus rocks!"

Adapting for . . .

Younger Children

Purchase smaller river rocks for your child and help them remember stories of Jesus doing miracles that they could illustrate on their rock. You may need to help him think of creative and simple ways to illustrate the story. (Example: Jesus fed thousands of people with a boy's sack lunch. Draw a sandwich and an apple.)

Teens

Have your teen read 1 Corinthians 15:12–20 and **Ask:** "What would happen if Easter were just a fairy tale and Christ actually did not rise from the grave?" (We would have no hope and be miserable.)

Prayer: *Dear God, today we celebrate that Jesus rose from the dead and gives us new life. We celebrate that your power still does miracles, just like that first Easter. Help us to look for your power working in our lives. In the risen Christ's name, Amen.*

INDEPENDENCE DAY—JULY 4

Main Point: Truth leads to freedom.

Materials Needed: Construction paper, scissors, markers, pencils, paper, clothes hanger, and fishing line

---

Warm-up

Ask: "What is 'independence' and why do we Americans celebrate it?" (Independence is the freedom of control of others. We celebrate our freedom from the rule of Great Britain when the Declaration of Independence was first adopted on July 4, 1776, and the United States of America was born.)

Bible Reading: Read aloud John 8:32:

And you will know the truth, and the truth will set you free.

What Does the Bible Say?

Say: "If we know the truth, we will be free."

Activity: The Pledge Hunt

Draw twelve five-point stars on construction paper (with pencil) and cut out with scissors. Make them at least two or three inches wide. Number them 1 to 12. Write the Pledge of Allegiance broken down into twelve phrases on the twelve stars:

(1) I pledge
(2) allegiance
(3) to the flag
(4) of the United States of America
(5) and to the Republic
(6) for which it stands
(7) one nation
(8) under God
(9) indivisible
(10) with liberty
(11) and justice
(12) for all

When the Freedom Stars are completed, collect them and hide them in the house or in the backyard. Make sure the kids don't see you hiding them. When they are hidden, come back to the kids and **Say:** "We are going to look for freedom today. Freedom isn't easy; we have to work at it. We have to look for it, and when we discover it, we have to keep it. We are going on a scavenger hunt for twelve stars that spell out our Pledge of Allegiance."

Family Discussion

What Should We Do?
After the hunt, gather the stars and arrange them in order.
Then lead a Discussion using the following:

Pledge of Allegiance/Meaning

(1) I pledge — A pledge is a promise.

(2) allegiance — I will be loyal and faithful.

(3) to the flag — Symbol of the ideals that made our country.

(4) of the United States of America — Though many states, we are all on the same team.

(5) and to the Republic — Everyone gets a vote.

(6) for which it stands — The flag represents the nation.

(7) one nation — Though many states, we are **one** nation.

(8) under God — People came here to worship God the way they wanted to.

(9) indivisible — Cannot be divided. Through challenges and disagreements, we chose to stay together.

(10) with liberty — We aren't prisoners of anyone. We are free.

(11) and justice — Fairness for everyone. All have rights.

(12) for all — Democracy includes everyone equally.

On the back of the stars, write the meaning. Then hang the stars with different lengths of fishing line from the hanger to make a *Freedom Star Mobile*. Display where you will see it.

Today's Slogan: *Memorize a patriotic poem.*

"My Country's Flag"
©2006 by Suzanne Smith, used with permision

Flag of my country
Reminds me that I'm free,
Free to be me!

Adapting for . . .

Younger Children
Draw the stars for her and help with the cutting. Explain the concepts of the pledge in terms she can understand.

Teens
Ask your teen to hide the Freedom Stars. For the Discussion, **Ask:** "What are some examples of two or three of the meanings?" (Example: "Give me an example of *allegiance*.")

Prayer: *Dear Father God, thank you for our country and the many blessings we enjoy: freedom, honor, the rights to vote and worship, and that everyone is valuable. Help us to build our lives, our family, and our country on your truth, because that will make us really free. In Jesus' name, Amen.*

MOTHER'S DAY

Main Point: Moms are our everyday heroes.

Materials Needed: Food for Mom's favorite breakfast or lunch, flowers, balloons, helium (or helium-filled balloons), string, streamers, recorded music and player, posters, markers, tape, and construction paper

Warm-up

Ask: "Today we are going to honor Mom. We want her to feel special and loved. What are some ways we can do that?"

Bible Reading: Read aloud Proverbs 31:28–29:

[A mother's] children stand and bless her. Her husband praises her. "There are many virtuous and capable women in the world, but you surpass them all!"

What Does the Bible Say?

Ask: "What does it mean to 'bless' Mom?" (Say nice things about her, show her respect and honor, etc.)

Activity: Pep Rally for Mom

Mothers do so much behind the scenes. Today is the day to make her the heroine! Serve her coffee or tea in bed (if this is for breakfast) along with some fresh fruit or a croissant. If it's for lunch, keep her in another part of the house while you prepare the food, so it will be a surprise. Have the kids help make the meal and set a fancy table with china, cloth napkins, candles, fresh flowers, etc.

Inflate balloons with helium and tie them together with string to make an arch. Hang streamers from the balloon arch. Mom will go through these (like a football team does at the start of a game).

Make several cheer posters, such as: "#1 MOM," "You Rock, Mom!" or "Hero of My Heart." (You can also use butcher paper for this, if you have it.) Make megaphones out of construction paper by rolling them into ice-cream cone shapes and taping them. Have each child decorate their megaphone by drawing pictures of what they appreciate about Mom and writing words of honor on their megaphone. When you are ready, start the music and have one person retrieve Mom. She is to walk through the arch as you cheer her with your megaphones and give her high-fives and pats on the back. Before the meal, have each child pray a short prayer about what they appreciate about Mom. During the meal, each child can read what he wrote on his megaphone, then present it to Mom as a gift. Conclude with Dad or the oldest child saying something like, "You surpass them all!" Kids do the cleanup, of course!

Family Discussion

What Should We Do?
The best time for this discussion might be before the pep rally.
1. **Ask:** "Why are we supposed to honor Mom?" (God commands us to; she deserves it.)
2. **Ask:** "What can we do on Mother's Day to really make it her day and not ours?"

Today's Slogan: "Mom is our hero!"

Adapting for . . .

Younger Children
Assist in making the megaphone and in drawing something that they like about Mom.

Teens
Enlist your teen to play peppy parade music on his musical instrument instead of playing the recorded music as Mom runs through the honor gauntlet.

Prayer: *Dear God, we rejoice in the mom you gave us. Thank you for her love, her faithfulness, and the hard work she does for our family. Help her to feel honored today. In Jesus' name, Amen.*

FATHER'S DAY

Main Point: A Godly father is worthy of honor.

Materials Needed: Twelve small gifts for Dad, paper bags, tape, marker, pen, pencil, and food for a barbeque or ice cream

Warm-up

Let Dad have some free time to lounge with his favorite beverage. During the preceding week, pull the kids aside and **Ask:** "What would make Dad feel special and loved for Father's Day?" See if you can incorporate some of the ideas into the following session.

Bible Reading: Read aloud Ephesians 6:1–3:

Children, obey your parents because you belong to the Lord, for this is the right thing to do. "Honor your father and mother." This is the first of the Ten Commandments that ends with a promise. And this is the promise: If you honor your father and mother, "you will live a long life, full of blessing."

What Does the Bible Say?

Ask: "What does it mean to obey your parents?" (Do as they tell you, or according to their rules.)

Activity: Hunter and Gatherer

Men like to hunt and gather, so let's give Dad a fun day of hunting outside! Purchase at least a dozen small gifts that Dad would like (golf balls, gift card to the home improvement store, razors, aftershave, favorite gum or candy, a DVD, gift card to his favorite restaurant, etc.) and wrap these in newspaper or brown sack paper. Number them and hide them in the backyard or in your neighborhood park. Keep a record of where you hide each one. Tell Dad, "For Father's Day we are going hunting; get ready to go." If he has some camouflage or blaze orange clothing, add some fun by having Dad wear it.

Provide a bag or tote for him to place his "game" as he gathers it. End everything with a barbeque or ice cream.

Family Discussion

What Should We Do?

1. **Ask:** "What part of *Hunter and Gatherer* did you enjoy?"
2. **Ask:** "Why is it important for kids to honor and obey their dads? What would happen if they didn't?" (They'd get in some kind of trouble or maybe even hurt themselves.)
3. **Ask:** "When you think of Dad, what are you thankful for?"

Today's Slogan: "Dad deserves my respect."

Adapting for . . .

Younger Children
Allow them to hide some of the gifts for Dad, and they can play *Cold, Warm, Hot*. "Cold" if Dad is far away from the gift; "warm" if he is getting closer; and "hot" if he's really close.

Teens
To extend the Discussion, **Ask:** "What is the link between honoring Dad and living a long life? Why is there a relationship between the two?" (To keep kids from living foolish lives that may be shortened.) "What are some ways teens can honor their dad, other than on Father's Day?"

Prayer: *Father God, we thank you for our dad. As we look at his life and his heart, we see you, our heavenly Father. Help us to appreciate him and cooperate with him and give him the respect he deserves, especially today as we celebrate him. In Jesus' name, Amen.*

Master Materials List

Here's a tip from one of the families that field tested these ideas: Get a cardboard box, decorate it, and write "Family Time Stuff" on the outside and stock it with basic materials. That way you'll have most of what you need for the sessions all ready to go. You might just need to get a few things for a particular session. Your basic stock includes: construction paper, scissors, tape, markers, string, yarn, butcher paper, poster board, pencils, pens, drawing paper, candles, balloons, and popcorn. The following shows the session number and what you will need for that session.

Session Materials

1. Socks, bowls, and string
2. A ball of yarn
3. Broomstick, twine, tape, and paper
4. Twelve small, smooth river stones and permanent markers
5. Popcorn and *Finding Nemo* movie
6. Park with playground equipment
7. Construction paper, scissors, markers, and tape
8. Baby food, spoon, juice, sipper cup, and bib
9. Butcher paper, scissors, and markers
10. Dictionary, a can of peaches, spoons, bowls, and can opener
11. Popcorn and *Father of the Bride* (or alternative) movie
12. Paper and pen
13. Car to drive to store
14. Fake check, butcher paper, pencils, rulers, crayons, and markers
15. Clear glass jar, walnut-sized rocks, marbles, and sand
16. Tape measure, painter's tape, chalk, broomstick, and recorded music and player

17. Wood blocks or books, bubble soaps and wands, pie tin, flex ties, and pipe cleaners
18. Play dress-up clothes, recorded music and player, pen, and paper
19. Newspaper, blindfold, and trash can
20. Neighborhood park
21. Cotton balls, tape, candy, purse, bathrobe, and broomstick
22. Shoeboxes, construction paper, glue, old magazines, and scraps of fabric
23. Shoelaces (or twine)
24. A sturdy kitchen chair
25. A bucket, washcloths, towel, water, soap, chair, and perfume
26. Popcorn, two cereal bowls, and *Toy Story* movie
27. Construction paper, tape, and markers
28. Sack lunch supplies, grocery gift card, or ingredients for cookies
29. Battery-powered toy or tool, nutrition bars, and sports drinks
30. Individually wrapped candies, ice-cream scoop, large bowl, and blindfold
31. One dollar and a dime for each family member, pen, and paper
32. Drawing paper, markers, shoebox, brown or black construction paper, glue, rope, bangles and knickknacks for decorations, and balsa wood strips (optional)
33. Popcorn, *Shrek 2* movie, old magazines, and scissors
34. Pen, paper, plastic grocery bags, clear contact paper, crayons, scissors, and nature stuff (leaves, sticks, etc.)
35. Ten pennies per child, a muffin tin, masking tape, marker, pen, and paper. Optional: cupcakes as a treat
36. Two small Ziploc-type bags, a pants hanger, masking tape, pen, and fifty pennies
37. Twine (or yarn), chair, and scissors

38. Empty cans, construction paper, markers, scissors, wrapping paper, and tape
39. Popcorn and *The Incredibles* movie
40. Paper, pen, construction paper, poster board, markers, scissors, tape, and glue. Optional: leather, canvas, wood, or ceramic clay
41. Family car and nearby museum
42. Extreme sports video
43. Wooden yardstick, construction paper, key ring, scissors, string, markers, tape, and drill
44. Large basket (or cardboard box), paper, and pen
45. Candle, matches, shoebox, wrapping paper, ribbon, and Christmas cards from friends. Optional: birthday cake and candles
46. Food for a meal, candles, sparkling cider, plastic champagne glasses, dessert, gold ribbons, silver seal stickers, and parchment-looking paper
47. Red or white wrapping paper, cardboard box with a lid, five yards of ribbon, a small wrapped gift for each family member, red or white construction paper, markers, and tape. (Advance preparation needed.)
48. Small clay pots, potting soil, a pony pack of flowers, trowel, acrylic paints and brushes, purple ribbon, orange juice, 7Up, juice glasses, and cut flowers or palm leaves
49. Large river rocks (at least softball size—one for each family member) and markers
50. Construction paper, scissors, markers, pencils, paper, clothes hanger, and fishing line
51. Food for breakfast or lunch, flowers, balloons, helium, string, streamers, recorded music and player, posters, markers, tape, and construction paper
52. Twelve small gifts for Dad, paper grocery bags, tape, marker, pen, pencil, and food for barbeque or ice cream

Also from Timothy Smith:

Timothy Smith challenges life's frantic pace and offers helpful solutions to slowing down and developing the perfect pulse for individual families. As families become increasingly busier, the stress puts a strain on relationships. But some active families have discovered a rhythmic pace, a heartbeat that works for them. *Connecting With Your Kids* is a stethoscope to listen to each individual's pulse and develop a cadence as a family benefiting everyone.

"The hurried lives we live rob families of the one thing that Jesus longed for us to have on a regular basis: rest— and the joy that a well-paced family is supposed to gain from it. In Connecting With Your Kids, *Tim Smith shows you the power of tempo when it comes to deeper and more satisfying relationships. It's a primer for how to slow down, savor the moments, while still getting ahead."*

—DR. TIM KIMMEL, Author of *Little House on the Freeway* and *Grace-Based Parenting*